W9-BCU-096

Young
John
Dewey

Young John Dewey

An Essay in American Intellectual History

Neil Coughlan

The University of Chicago Press
Chicago and London

The University of Chicago Press, Chicago 60637
The University of Chicago Press, Ltd., London
© 1975 by The University of Chicago
All rights reserved. Published 1975
Printed in the United States of America

Library of Congress Cataloging in Publication Data

Coughlan, Neil, 1938–
  Young John Dewey: an essay in American intellectual history.

  Bibliography: p.
  Includes index.
  1. Dewey, John, 1859–1952.   I. Title.
B945.D44C63   191 [B]   74-33519
ISBN 0-226-11604-2

Neil Coughlan taught history at Wesleyan
University (Connecticut) from 1968 to 1974.
He is now studying law at Yale Law School.

To Philippa, admiringly

Contents

Preface

"The Metaphysical Assumptions of Materialism," John Dewey titled the first piece he wrote for publication. It hardly augured a body of confessional prose, and indeed his early writings were to be focused unwaveringly on the impersonal issues of epistemology, metaphysics, and ethics. Yet as I followed Dewey through some years of the abstract and difficult prose of Hegelianism and watched it change into something else, a wholly new American philosophy, I sensed that the writing had another level to it and that I was traveling in the company of a young man who through his philosophy was also addressing what we clumsily call personal issues—that Dewey as much as any of us was asking, "What shall I do with my life?" "Where shall I find meaning?" And I felt certain that the way to tell the story of the creation of this new philosophy was to tell with it the story of the young man who created it.

Needless to say, John Dewey's path was his own. But it signified a crisis in his culture, nineteenth-century American evangelical Protestantism, and the appearance in America of a new institution, the modern university. These two contexts shaped Dewey and they shaped his philosophy. Following this side of the story brought me into several apparent bypaths—into the lives of such men as George Sylvester Morris and Newman Smyth and George Herbert Mead. Obviously, I don't see these as bypaths at all. I hope the reader will find in them what I did.

N. C.

Acknowledgments

I incurred many debts of gratitude in the course of writing this book. Dr. Jo Ann Boydston and her staff at the Center for Dewey Studies are providing a matchless service for people interested in Dewey, and they were unfailingly kind and helpful to me. For permission to quote from unpublished correspondence I am grateful to Mrs. Henry C. Mead, Dr. Irene Tufts Mead, John U. Nef, Henry C. Torrey, and the Center for Dewey Studies. I was assisted also by many libraries, particularly by the staffs of the University of Chicago Library, the Michigan Historical Collections, and the Olin Library at Wesleyan University. I was aided by grants from the graduate school of the University of Wisconsin, the Newberry Library, and Wesleyan University. I am especially grateful to the latter institution for its wise and generous policy of support for scholarship.

Dorothy Hay's kindness and wise judgment helped me along the way, and I had the skilled and intelligent assistance of Rebecca Gagnon in the final preparation of the manuscript. Robert McCaul of the School of Education at the University of Chicago made available to me his unpublished manuscript on young Dewey. I am indebted to friends and colleagues in the Wesleyan Department of History and elsewhere, but to none so much as to Louis Mink, of the Wesleyan Department of Philosophy, who suggested numerous improvements in the manuscript over a period of five years. Writing a book, I found, is as much a test of morale as of intellect; for encouragement I am particularly grateful to my father, Patrick J. Coughlan, and to Michael Michaelson of New York City.

In torts law there is a useful category called "but for" cause. But for my dissertation director at the University of Wisconsin, Professor William R. Taylor (now of the Department of History

xii   Acknowledgments

at SUNY, Stony Brook) this book would never have been so much as started. He made history an exciting and rewarding pursuit. My greatest personal debt is acknowledged in the dedication.

Young
John
Dewey

1   Early Years

Dewey was born on October 20, 1859, in Burlington, Vermont. His father, Archibald Sprague Dewey, a north Vermont farm boy who became a reasonably successful town grocer and later a tobacconist, was a handsome, outgoing, witty man, then about forty-eight years of age, said "to sell more goods and collect fewer bills than any other man in town." Dewey's mother, Lucina Rich Dewey, was almost twenty years younger than her husband, and better-born. She had come from a prominent and well-to-do Vermont family: her grandfather had been a United States congressman for ten years, her father had served in the Vermont legislature, and all her brothers were college men. It was the sixth year of her marriage to Archibald Dewey, and John was the third child (there were to be four, all boys). Nine months before Dewey was born, on the evening of January 17, the oldest son, two and half years of age, had fallen backward into a pail of scalding water. His parents had tried to treat his burns, swathing him in "sweet oil and cotton batting," but the dressing caught fire on the child and he died the next morning. His name was John Archibald. Presumably, Dewey was named after his dead brother, though he was not given a middle name.[1] Early in 1861, a year and a half after Dewey was born, his father answered Lincoln's first call for volunteers and enlisted as quartermaster of the First Vermont Cavalry. He remained on active duty until some time after the end of the war. In 1864, after three years of this separation, Dewey's mother sold the family house and brought the children down to Virginia, where Archibald was stationed. It was not until 1867 that the family returned to Burlington and settled down again.

Lucina Dewey seems by all accounts to have been an unusual woman. Her family had been in New England since the seventeenth century, and by her generation their religion had evolved into a comparatively cool, urbane Universalism. Sometime in her late adolescence, however, Lucina had gone out to Ohio to visit another branch of the family, also Universalists. There she had made a new friend, another girl, and with her had begun to go to the local revival meetings. Her relatives wrote home to Vermont, warning her father to send for her, but he wasn't quick enough. Lucina was converted, and she came back to Vermont a pious evangelical.

Her independence and intensity of inner experience can hardly have been much softened by her subsequent marriage to Archibald Dewey. He was too much of a man's man. His success as a merchandiser and good record as quartermaster seem to have been more a function of his easygoing good sense and geniality ("Hams and Cigars—Smoked and Unsmoked. A. S. Dewey," read his advertisement) than of any great drive. He was a churchgoer, but one like any other man in town, a liberal Congregationalist and no zealot. As for his ambitions for his three sons, he expressed the hope that at least one of them would be a mechanic and left it at that.

Had Archibald Dewey had a bit more ambition (had he at least *understood* that Lucina's sons would have to go to college, as had her brothers), had he been a younger man or perhaps a little more meditative or pious to make a better soul mate for Lucina, theirs might have been an ideal marriage, these qualities serving to bring husband and wife close enough to make his geniality and sociability accessible to Lucina and to take the edge off her intensity. Archibald was who he was, however, and things do not seem to have worked out this way. Furthermore, the circumstances and events of the first decade of their marriage—Archibald's going off soldiering and leaving Lucina with two small sons, the elder only three, and a third soon to be born—worked against such a growing-together and, if anything, led Lucina to rely even more on her own resources and perceptions.

When Dewey spoke about his mother, he remembered a woman of great piety, strict with her sons, given to asking them—even in the presence of others—whether they were "right with Jesus."[2] Her religiosity was not at all a compensation for any personal coldness, however. She was solicitous and attentive, and her sons seem to have been deeply loved. (In later years Lucina acquired a considerable local reputation as a confidante and counselor of young men.)[3] It was she who taught her sons their prayers; she took them to Sunday services; and when it came time for John to join the church, she wrote the petition for her eleven-year-old son:

> I think I love Christ and want to obey him. I have thought for some time I should like to unite with the church. Now, I want to more, for it seems one way to confess Him, and I should like to remember Him at the Communion.[4]

In bringing John to church, his mother may have had some misgivings, for the Calvinism that was preached in the Burlington Congregational Church was not the "hot" religion that had converted her. It *was* evangelical—a religion of the bible, not a disguised rationalism—but it was a quiet, refined, liberal orthodoxy, more intellectual than experiential (or, in the word of the revivalists, experimental). By exposing young John to the sermons of the minister, Lewis Ormond Brastow, Lucina, whether she sensed it or not, was introducing her son to the other pole between which and her piety Dewey would string his personal experience and growth. Until he was almost thirty years old, the greater part of Dewey's intellectual life was concerned with mediating between that core of evangelicalism that his mother had given him and life as men live it, particularly the intellectual life of the late nineteenth century. In the person of Brastow and in the cerebral qualities of his religion Dewey quite likely encountered his first model for this pursuit.

The pressures on the sons of women like Lucina Rich Dewey would have been considerable. This is not to say, however, that there would have been anything necessarily destructive about them. Quite the contrary. Mrs. Dewey almost certainly was a psychically healthy woman. She had great drives, but she had avenues for them that were socially prized: work, prayer, benevolence, maternity (she took in her brother's family when he lost his wife in the early 1860s), and not unattainable goals in this world for her family. She achieved a real stability—dynamic, to be sure, and not placid, but a stability nevertheless. It was the same with her marriage. Her life with (and, during the Civil War, away from) Archibald Dewey may have left her with a certain spiritual loneliness, a slight disappointment in his limited ambitions, and an exaggerated sense of the need for self-reliance, but this did not make for a bad marriage. She and Archibald had considerable common ground. He was a respected member of the community; the family had for their friends such men as James Burrill Angell and Matthew Buckham, prominent faculty members and successive presidents of the University of Vermont (which is situated in Burlington). Archibald was reasonably well read (Shakespeare, Milton, Lamb, and Thackeray were his favorites), and he was a masculine, kindly, and not irreligious man.

The home life of the boys, then, was not morbid, but, in the person of their mother, it was demanding. John and his surviving elder brother, Davis Rich Dewey, the two sons who had the strength of ego to stand up to its demands and the talents to live up to them, flourished in that environment. Davis went on to become a prominent academic economist, editor of the *American Economic Review* until he was past eighty, and a man with an "extraordinarily pleasant temperament." The last son, however, Charles Miner Dewey, seems to have opted out at some point, to have assumed the role of family scamp and thus freed himself to go off and perhaps to imitate the easygoing person of his father. He failed out of the University of Vermont in his freshman year and left for the west coast, where he went into business and had only infrequent contacts with his brothers.

In a brief autobiographical sketch he wrote when he was sixty years old, Dewey referred somewhat obscurely to "an inward laceration" inflicted on him by "a heritage of New England culture" with its "divisions by way of isolation of self from the world, of soul from body, of nature from God."[5] This may or may not be an accurate rendering of the impact of Calvinism on the human spirit in general, but in this case it is plain that it was elicited at least in part by Dewey's memory of himself as a shy, self-conscious little boy who at some level had been taught that the world is not to be taken at face value, that it is not as benevolent as it might look, not just a natural setting made for romping—a boy, in short, who had absorbed his mother's view of the world. John, like his brother Davis, was a quiet child, a follower at play, not a leader. This quietness and reserve may also have been a sign that many of his energies were being absorbed in sorting out another relationship. Finding a self while under the eye of a strong, deep, child-centered woman with an exact and rigid notion of the way things should be cannot have been an easy business, and it must have required of young Dewey a sort of delicate and largely unconscious diplomacy to nurture the makings of a private self while at the same time responding to his mother's attentiveness and subscribing to her values. The final fruits of such a process, if all went well, would not be a blithesomeness, but it could be in the long run a carefully constructed, sensitive, stable, even very powerful ego—a clear "sense of one's self." In Dewey's case this was precisely the outcome.

In the meanwhile, however, there were costs. Certain types of spontaneity and social ease were lost or never emerged. Happily, Dewey had the outdoors and a small, tight circle of friends: his brother Davis, his cousin John Rich, who was being raised by the Deweys, and the two Buckham boys. They led a life that was

> simple and healthful but somewhat isolated from the current of life about them. John and Davis were book-worms and John was bashful, with the tendency to self-consciousness which so often accompanies that trait. . . . They were younger than other boys in their grades, though not markedly precocious, and took little interest in games. However, they were unconscious of any unhappy differences between themselves and their mates, satisfied with their own company in work and play.[6]

When he was fifteen years old, Dewey graduated from the local high school and entered the University of Vermont. In reality, the "university" was a very small New England college. During Dewey's four years there it had eight or so faculty members (most of them well known to the Dewey family) and fewer than a hundred students. Dewey himself graduated in a class of eighteen, which included in its number his brother Davis and John Rich. Dewey took the classical curriculum, as did most of the students, and his first two years were given over to Greek, Latin, ancient history, analytical geometry, and calculus. His intellectual awakening, however, occurred at the beginning of his junior year. He was taught geology and zoology that year by a professor who structured his presentations on the theory of evolution; similarly, the physiology course he took used the text written by T. H. Huxley, one of Darwin's earliest champions.

Sixty years later he still recalled the impact the book had had on him.[7] Dewey's reading changed, also. His first two years' borrowings from the university library had been standard and utterly orthodox, going no farther from New England church culture than *The Mill on the Floss*. In the fall of his junior year, however, he turned to Matthew Arnold's books and to the little group of English reviews that were devoted to serious discussion of the issues of the age, most particularly the implications of science and evolution for traditional religion. He became interested in Comte and in his senior year read heavily in Herbert Spencer.[8] These new interests were further reinforced in the classroom by the "senior-year course," to which Dewey later paid tribute, with its introductions to various branches of speculative and social philosophy.

Dewey graduated from the University of Vermont in 1879 and decided to teach high school. He had trouble finding a position, however—his youth and inexperience, he recalled, told against him. Probably his shyness hurt him, too. He never completely conquered this trait, and in those days it was acute.[9] High-school teaching was still a strenuous business in the 1870s, and in many rural schools only the skilled disciplinarian could so much as keep order, much less teach anything. All the school's students were likely to be in one classroom, they ranged in age from late childhood to twenty or more, and parental support of the teacher was often minimal. Dewey's reticent intellectuality did not augur well for such work. Finally, at the end of the summer, a relative who was principal of a high school in Oil City, Pennsylvania, telegraphed an offer to Dewey and he took it.

It is likely that his two-year tenure in this position was personally difficult for Dewey. He can hardly have seen high-school teaching as anything more than an interim occupation, a way of buying some time to take stock and decide what to make of himself. A lonely moment in anybody's life, it may have been a very bad time indeed for Dewey, boarding alone in a raw, ugly little industrial city and far from the home and brother and two or three friends he had been so close to.

He later remembered that it was sometime in these two years, "one evening while he sat reading," that he had his one mystical experience. It came by way of "an answer to that question which still worried him: whether he really meant business when he prayed": "It was not a very dramatic mystic experience. There was no vision, not even a definable emotion—just a supremely blissful feeling that his worries were over. . . . 'I've never had any doubts since then, nor any beliefs.' "[10] What Dewey had experienced here was in all likelihood a particularly vivid moment in the transformation of his religious faith from the unnameable, anxiety-ridden incubus it can be in the worst moments of childhood and adolescence into something more manageable, something whose demands might be satisfied by human transactions. Dewey was overeager in remembering this moment as dating the end of his religious "beliefs" (his Christianity was very much alive for another five years at least), but he was accurate to the extent that he was indicating that his eventual departure from religion was the result of a series of such naturalizing steps whereby what had passed for transcendent and supernatural was discovered to be a mystification of something finite and natural.

During his time in Oil City, Dewey kept reading in philosophy and in the spring of the second year wrote an essay, "The Metaphysical Assumptions of Materialism," in which he sought to demonstrate that philosophical materialism is logically untenable, that only by adopting a covertly antimaterialist stance can one assert it at all. He sent his article to William Torrey Harris, editor of the *Journal of Speculative Philosophy*, the only exclusively philosophical periodical then being published in the United States. He enclosed with the article an anxious little note introducing himself to Harris. "I suppose you must be troubled with many inquiries of this sort," it concluded,

> yet if it would not be too much to ask, I should be glad to know your opinion on it, if you make no use of it. An opinion as to whether you considered it to show ability enough of any kind to warrant my putting much of my time on that sort of subject would be thankfully received, and, as I am a young man in doubt as to how to employ my reading hours, might be of much advantage. I do not wish to ask too much of your time and attention however.

> Yours very truly,
> JOHN DEWEY[11]

Dewey did not receive an answer from Harris until late

October. In the meantime he had come back to Vermont and a job as the only teacher in a small high school near Burlington. He had a wretched time of it; the older boys among the school's thirty-five students ran amok. Many years later an old lady who had been in the class could recall only "how terribly the boys behaved, and how long and fervent was the prayer with which he [Dewey] opened each school day."[12]

Dewey made an arrangement that year for private study in philosophical German and the classics of philosophy with Professor Henry A. P. Torrey, who had been his philosophy teacher at the University of Vermont. Dewey would do his reading and the two of them would go for long walks together and talk about it. It was an arrangement that favored intellectual intimacy (a potential reinforced no doubt by its happy contrast with the chaos Dewey faced each day in his classroom), and, as Torrey must have sensed, his young student was taking him very seriously as a figure. Dewey already had it in mind to become a philosopher, and his interests—the areas of epistemology and metaphysics where the battle between theism and materialism was being fought—corresponded exactly with Torrey's. The attraction had another basis, too—one that is worth mentioning because it had to do with a pattern that, since it recurred in young Dewey's life, helps to explain the personal and philosophical directions he took.

It was probably clear to Dewey when he was still quite young, a child, that his father was not to be a complete life-model for him. Not that he did not love his father, for he must have enjoyed in him what everyone enjoyed, finding delight in his stories, security in his masculinity, and respite from Lucina's strictness in his sensible indulgence. Dewey's early dissimilarity from his father, however—his retiring, ruminative personality as a child, his absorption of his mother's religion and ideals, and, eventually, his understanding that he would be no grocer or tobacconist but a college man—left him with a pronounced openness to a certain kind of masculine figure, a man of intellectuality, piety, and distinction in the community, a man, that is to say, who would personify the virtues and aspirations Dewey's mother had held up to the boy and at the same time do for him what his mother could not: represent the translation of those ideals into a form of public masculine stature and achievement. The circle of Dewey family friends was in large part made up of men of this type: Brastow, the minister of the Congregational Church; James Burrill Angell, president of the University of Vermont from 1866 until 1871 (and thereafter president of the University of Michigan); his successor, Matthew Buckham, former minister, professor of political and social philosophy at the university, and the father of Dewey's closest boyhood friends; John Ellsworth Goodrich, professor of rhetoric and languages, university librarian, and chaplain of the First Vermont Cavalry, which Archibald Dewey served as quartermaster.

Torrey, to whom Dewey now turned, was from the same mold. Born in 1837 in Massachusetts, Torrey had graduated from the University of Vermont in 1858 and, after teaching school for a few years, had gone to study for the ministry at Union Theological Seminary in New York. After a short stint in the pastorate of a Congregational Church in Vergennes, Vermont, he was invited in 1868 to the chair of intellectual and moral philosophy at Vermont, which had been vacated by the death of his uncle, Joseph Torrey. He held the post until his own death in 1903. Torrey was a teacher, not a writer, and over the years he published little: a book of excerpts from Descartes and a rare few articles and reviews. All his life he held to a liberal evangelical orthodoxy. [13]

There exists considerable confusion about Torrey's personal philosophical standpoint. He was best known as an expounder of Kant; yet his most famous classroom lectures are unmistakably intuitionalist, and years later John Dewey also remembered him as a Scottish common-sense realist and moral intuitionalist. There is nothing to be gained, however, from trying to resolve Torrey into one or the other, for it is most probable that he was both a Kantian and an intuitionalist and that his philosophical inconsistency was in the service of a larger personal and situational consistency.

On most technical philosophical issues Torrey seems to have been a Kantian. Kant had to confront the fact that Hume's criticisms had laid waste the traditional philosophical bases of Christianity. Hume had examined man's notion that he is a "person" or has a "self" and found it to be nothing more than a belief based solely on the coexistence in the same time and place of a congeries of subjective impressions or perceptions. He found nothing to justify our belief that we each have a "soul"—a real, substantial, spiritual entity. The other foundations of Christianity had also fared badly in his examination. The classic proofs for the existence of God, he found, were based on man's conviction that causality really prevails in the natural order and, like that conviction, are ultimately founded on the pathetic fallacy—the wish become the thought. Further, Hume's denial of these two premises—of a substantial soul and of the demonstrability of the existence of God—overthrew the traditional bases for an objective code of morality and for the belief in a life after death. Kant's strategy in responding to Hume was first (in his *Critique of Pure Reason*) to examine the nature and limitations of man's speculative or scientific knowledge. There he found that, much as Hume had concluded, man cannot know what things are really like in themselves, because to think is to mold: the only way the mind is able to experience is to first transform sense data by subjecting them to the mind's own categories. Therefore, the mind operates at one remove from reality; it never encounters the thing as it is in itself (this Kant called the "noumenon"). But where Hume in denying this type of "substantial" knowledge to man had assumed that human perception is passive, that it merely *receives* impressions, Kant argued that in subjecting things to its own categories the mind reveals itself as an intrinsically *active* force; further, the unity and continuity of the mind's consciousness and experience argue to the transcendental (i.e., prior to experience and not subject to being tested by it) unity of the perceiving self. In other words, they argue to the reality of the noumenal self.

Of the beleaguered canons of Christian orthodoxy, *The Critique of Pure Reason* really rescued only one: the existence of the human soul. However, and this was at the heart of Kant's strategy, it showed the limitations of scientific knowledge: that it can say nothing about extrasensible reality. In its incapacity to know the thing-in-itself, scientific knowledge can neither prove nor disprove propositions about such "noumenal" matters as the existence of God, the freedom of the will, or the immortality of the soul. These issues can be spoken to only in the realm of what Kant called "practical reason," that is, in the realm of rational *action*. Here, Kant said, the first datum is that all men have an immediate consciousness of a moral impulse, an impulse to do good. The implementation of this moral urge necessarily involves men in the practical hypothesis that they are free to do so. Ultimately, Kant argued, it also involves them of necessity in the hypotheses that God exists and that the soul is immortal. The rejection of any of these hypotheses would involve a man in living a contradiction: acting as though he had free will while insisting that he did not have it, etc.

The appeal of this Kantianism to Torrey should need no explanation. On the matter of the human person, it left Hume and the later associationalists hoist by their own petard, showing that their analysis of human experience made it only the *more* certain that man has a soul. The other key claims of theism—hard pressed in Torrey's day by the attacks of the Darwinians and Spencerians—it at least removed to safe, high ground by establishing that scientific findings are able to say nothing, pro or con, about the supersensible realities of divine truth: these are above proof.

Yet, though Torrey seems to have gratefully accepted these features of Kant's philosophy, he stopped short of taking the system whole. As can be seen, it is an integral and unavoidable tenet of a consistent Kantianism that the mind is constitutionally ignorant of the thing-in-itself: the mind can know the *phenomena* but not the *noumenon*. Really, this is where Kant's philosophy started—he was convinced by Hume's argument that what we know is, not the thing itself, but our ideas of the thing. Torrey, however, would not have it. John Wright Buckham, Dewey's boyhood friend who grew up to be a minister and professor of religion, remembered that Torrey would not

> assent to Kant's skepticism concerning the validity of our
> rational faculties, even in the interest of moral reason—as the
> writer well remembers when as a pupil of Professor Torrey,
> in the callowness of youth, he sought to win his approval of
> the Kantian agnosticism [meaning, of course, *noumenal* ag-
> nosticism, not theological agnosticism].[14]

Instead, Torrey invoked Scottish common-sense realism and its companion doctrine, moral intuitionalism. From the standpoint of technical philosophy it was a much simpler and less sophisticated system than Kant's. It denied the first principle of Hume's epistemology, that our knowledge begins with simple ideas or impressions and that it is built up by combining and comparing them. Rather, such Scottish philosophers as Reid held that those simple ideas (the greenness of a tree, say) are *not* what we immediately perceive but are the products of an analysis subsequent to the original perception. We don't see merely a congeries of discrete qualities—greenness, tallness, solidity—and then give the coincidence of these qualities the name "tree"; rather, the original perception is the perception *of the tree itself*, of its substance and of the fact that it exists. These judgments are in the perception itself; Hume had the natural order backwards. Reid pointed out that his conclusion jibed exactly with the common sense of mankind, that this is how men ordinarily understand perception.

It was the same, the Scottish philosophers said, with what they called the "principles of common sense." All men are gifted with a primary intuitive understanding that qualities such as color, and so forth, do inhere in an actual substance, the tree or whatever; that everything that begins to exist must have a cause; and that the nature of the cause can be inferred from the nature of its effects. Likewise, they extended their principles into the realm of morals: men have an intuitive grasp of right and wrong.

The common-sense philosophy, if true, would reestablish the entire traditional philosophical defense of Christianity. Since men actually do intuit the substance, the real nature of things, they can see that man and nature both are contingent, caused beings. (Hume and Kant had held that we can say only that cause-and-effect is a way the mind has of seeing the world, not that it is a relation intrinsic in things themselves.) If man and nature as they now exist are caused beings, and if what caused them was itself a caused being, ultimately the whole chain must lead back to an original Uncaused Cause. Its nature? Effect resembles cause, and the obvious order and teleology in nature argue to a Designing Intelligence—the personal God of Christianity. In fine, the Scotch realism held that man "can directly read eternal truths in the simplest perceptions"; and H. A. P. Torrey, in subscribing to it, was holding out for the natural theology that Hume and Kant had dismissed as impossible.

How and why Torrey came to hold simultaneously two contradictory philosophies it would be hard to say with precision, but some elements in the situation are plain enough. We have it on the word of a friend of his, E. H. Griffin, that his Kantianism served Torrey as a way of coming to terms with evolutionary science. He used it to establish that science's inquiry into the origin and nature of things is at a different level from religion's. Science is limited to the phenomenal realm; it cannot threaten religion's authority, which pronounces on the noumenal—the thing-in-itself, its *metaphysical* import.

The problem with Kantianism, however, as far as Torrey was concerned, was that it limited *all* human intellectual understanding to the phenomenal realm. That is to say, Kant held metaphysics impossible. No one, neither scientist nor philosopher, can get to the thing-in-itself. It was this that Torrey found unacceptable, for besides being a man of religion, he was a philosopher and a metaphysician by trade, a professor "of Mental and Moral Philosophy."

To understand the difficulties Torrey would have encountered in holding to a consistent Kantianism, it is necessary only to limn some of the principal features of his personal situation. To begin with, it would be a mistake to think that his position as "Professor of Mental and Moral Philosophy" was tantamount to the position of a philosophy professor in a modern university. The latter, presumably, is fulfilling his calling if he lets logic lead him where it will—it is the only dynamic and authority to which he is responsible. Torrey's principal responsibility was to the New England church culture. As his easy transfer from pulpit to chair of philosophy had symbolized, his duties were to demonstrate *how* philosophy and human reason tended to support the teachings of Scripture (certainly not to ask *whether* they did). He was to be the philosophical arm of the preaching ministry. Kantianism ill lent itself to such duties; instead of the world preached from the pulpits—a stage set by God, a universe and a human history in which can be read, however obscurely, something of Him and His purposes—Kant's philosophy leaves an utterly mysterious nature, one that evidences no order or purpose to the human mind. This was poor material for a lifetime of sermons. What Torrey needed, his friend Griffin wrote, was a way to philosophize about

the ideal significance of things, seeking to determine their essential character and meaning as entering into human experience and as involving human destiny. This, not being an inquiry in the field of objective phenomena to which methods of experiment and external observations are applicable, is to be decided introspectively, on grounds of reason and self-consciousness, aesthetic and ethical feeling, speculative insight. [15]

Needless to say, this description of Torrey's noumenal ruminations would do equally well as the definition of a standard sermon. It must have been for reasons like this that Torrey would leave Kantianism as soon as he had used it to put the scientists in their place and would then turn to Scottish common-sense realism and moral intuitionalism.

It was the same story in his own classroom. His most famous offering was his "Mansfield Course," lectures in which he would address himself to the great mountain that overlooked the university, examining it first as an empirical phenomenon and then as "a mental concept." [16] Exactly what he said in this second part of the discussion we do not know, but Lewis Feuer has remarked about it that Torrey "accepted the truth of moral intuition in a more ultimate sense than Kant's practical reason would allow." [17] And well he might. Had he not, his course would have had to stop with the *scientific* description of Mount Mansfield, and there would have been no second half to it.

Clearly there were many points at which the direction of Torrey's philosophy was dictated not by its own logic but by forces external to it: his prior commitment to his beliefs and his office. Dewey recalled that Torrey had once said to him, "Undoubtedly pantheism is the most satisfactory form of metaphysics intellectually, but it goes counter to religious faith"; as Dewey said, Torrey "never really let his mind go." [18] In Torrey's culture, however, not letting his mind go was a virtue, and Torrey and men like him were honored for it. Torrey himself was memorialized by fellow ministers and religious philosophers as something of a saint, a man of courage, "intellectual refinement," and "gentleness and high purposes." Most of all, though, it was his judicial mental reserve that they dwelt on: "He was a great truth lover, burning with quiet ardor for the truth—yet never with a hectic or superficial flame." [19]

The day would come when Dewey could see Torrey as having been "constitutionally timid," a man who let an inner conflict prevent "his native capacity from coming to full fruition," but it

was a long time in coming. [20] Certainly during the year that he
studied privately with Torrey there was very little detachment in
Dewey's view of the older man. The eclectic nature of Torrey's
philosophy and its irresolution no doubt precluded a formal
discipleship on the part of Dewey; but as for the spirit of Torrey's
thought and the ethic on which it was based, young Dewey made
them his own.

Toward the end of October of that year, though he still had not
heard from W. T. Harris about the essay he had sent him six
months earlier, Dewey submitted another article to the *Journal of
Speculative Philosophy*, this one a criticism of Spinoza's pantheism. The next day, by coincidence, Harris's acceptance of the first
article arrived in the mail, accompanied apparently by an
encouraging appraisal of Dewey's abilities in philosophy. Dewey
wrote back:

> Yours of the 17th inst. is at hand. Thanks for your favorable
> opinion. I should be glad to have you print it [the first article,
> "The Metaphysical Assumptions of Materialism"], if you
> desire. As I do not take the Journal myself, if you do print it, I
> should be glad to have a copy or two. Yesterday, previous to
> receiving your communication, I sent another article to you on
> the Pantheism of Spinoza. I should be glad to have you make
> any use of that which you see fit. I am a young man, having
> studied philosophy but a comparatively short time and do not
> particularly care for pay for any articles that you think worthy
> of print.
>
> Yours Sincerely,
> JOHN DEWEY[21]

Shortly thereafter, with Torrey's encouragement, Dewey applied
for a graduate fellowship at the Johns Hopkins University.
Though he came recommended by Torrey to the Johns Hopkins
Department of Philosophy for his "marked predilection for
metaphysics" and his "high character and devotion to philosophy,"[22] Dewey did not win any of the fellowships, nor did he get
the lower-paying scholarship he next applied for. Finally, he
borrowed the money from an aunt and enrolled at the university
in September 1882 to study philosophy and psychology.

When Dewey came to Johns Hopkins in the fall of 1882, the university was in its early heyday, and many of the names on its rolls as faculty and graduate students during the two years he studied there would later be listed among the greats of the American academic world. Though Dewey took Charles Sanders Peirce's courses and spoke up in forum with Woodrow Wilson, his central intellectual experience in graduate school was almost exclusively a function of his association with two men, George Sylvester Morris, who taught him philosophy, and Granville Stanley Hall, who taught him psychology. Young Dewey could not have devised a more charged or significant pairing of masters, for Morris and Hall were engaged in a professional conflict whose outcome would reveal much about the future of the American university and about American intellectual life for the next thirty years. It was a conflict, also, that should be understood if one would understand Dewey and the identity he eventually established for himself.

∽

George Morris was born in 1840 in Norwich, Vermont, of a Congregational family that had come from England to Massachusetts in 1636. His father was a tanner, a town businessman of considerable enterprise and success, and the most militant abolitionist and temperance reformer in the area. The son was educated in the local school and at Kimball Union Academy, fifteen miles away in Meriden, New Hampshire. In 1857 he entered Dartmouth College, and after his graduation with high honors in 1861 he took a position as principal of Royalton Academy in Royalton, Vermont. At the end of the school year he resigned, intending to study for the ministry; but the Civil War intervened, and despite his physical frailty he enlisted in the Second Vermont Brigade. In the autumn of 1863 he was mustered out and again turned to teaching, this time as tutor in Greek and mathematics at Dartmouth, in order to earn the money to underwrite his seminary training. The following year, at long last, he enrolled at Union Theological Seminary (this was just about the date that H. A. P. Torrey was finishing his studies there). [1]

Sometime during his two years of study at Union, Morris suffered the onset of what would be a protracted crisis of faith, a temptation to agnosticism and materialism, occasioned apparently by his reading of Hume and other British empiricists. It seems to have been an extraordinarily painful trial, and the Union community at large was apparently aware of it. It was still unresolved when, at the end of his second year of divinity studies, Morris left America for a projected three years of study in Germany. [2] Henry Boynton Smith, one of the seminary's most distinguished professors, a man who had himself studied theology and philosophy at German universities, had advised Morris to go there, and it seems to have been understood between Smith and his student that this would mean a slight change of vocation, from minister to professor of philosophy.

In Europe Morris studied for a while with two philosophers recommended to him by Professor Smith, Hermann Ulrici of Halle and Friedrich A. Trendelenburg of Berlin. He then wandered from one center of culture to another in Germany, Switzerland, France, Austria, and Italy, his moods varying from elation to extreme depression. His restlessness did not abate, and in August 1868 he allowed in a letter home that he was "so anxious to be earning something and to be settled in a fixed occupation."[3] He had apparently given up completely any thoughts of the ministry or of teaching in the seminary and was toying with the idea of staying in Europe as American consul in one of the major cities. He wrote home, instructing his father to see if this couldn't be arranged through the family's political connections, but apparently nothing came of it. That autumn he left Europe.

Morris came home to a wretchedly unhappy situation. His former fiancée, who had broken off their engagement that summer, while Morris was still in Europe, because "he had grown so learned and changed so much in his religious opinions, that she was afraid of him," refused to see him again. [4] Then he found that he could obtain no position even remotely commensurate with his learning or ambitions. No college or university was interested in hiring him. Finally, in the face of an alternative of soul-destroying idleness in a Vermont town, Morris took a job as resident tutor for the children of a prominent New York banker, Jesse Seligman.

Morris's troubles with his fiancée and with the academic world were of a piece: the word had spread that he was in danger of losing his faith. Morris's orthodoxy was suspect in the tight little circle of the respectable American colleges, and there did not as yet exist an American university world free from such sectarianism and able to step in and offer Morris the university lectureship or chair of philosophy he might have hoped for had he been, say, a German making his way in Europe during these years. What few American universities existed were for the most part inchoate, still trying to distinguish themselves from the dominant college-seminary model of higher education. This attempt to justify the university ideal frequently put presidents and faculty in an extremely delicate position before both their consciences and their public on the matter of maintaining Christian orthodoxy and moral respectability. Only to the degree that they were able to allay fears in this area were they free to pursue excellence in other areas according to their own lights. Their response was a predictable one; generally, they fostered supinely orthodox chapels and philosophy departments. When finally, in 1870, after he had spent two years as a family tutor, the University of Michigan sought to hire Morris, it asked him to fill the chair of modern languages and literature. Morris accepted the position. Typically, the chair of philosophy during these years was held by a Methodist preacher whose formal schooling had ended at age thirteen but who was a gifted speaker and a person of great moral earnestness. The students "took an uplift" from his classes.

The unhappiness of Morris's situation was reflected in his behavior at Michigan. During the first years of his tenure there the students found him shy and distant, and he "took little, if any, part in the general affairs of the university." [5] In the entire period from 1870 till 1882 he gave perhaps three public speeches, and these few he gave with great reluctance.

Although Morris left no personal documents from this period of his life, his few publications during these years give some indication of what was happening to him. In 1873, his third year at Michigan, he wrote a summary of the philosophy of Friedrich Trendelenburg, the man he had studied under in Berlin in the winter of 1867–68. It was the best thing he would write for a long time; perhaps it was the best he ever wrote.[6] Its subject was a philosopher who had established a relaxed and mutually supportive relationship between modern empirical science and traditional theistic epistemology and metaphysics. Trendelenburg had dispelled Hume's and Kant's epistemological challenges by suggesting that instead of deciding beforehand—before philosophy begins!—what is knowable or unknowable, we would do better to examine carefully mankind's assumption that we can know reality for what it is. This assumption deserves to be taken seriously because the evidence seems to support it. Pure mathematics is borne out by applied mathematics, physics by engineering; thus modern science and our growing control over nature seem to indicate that we do know nature. How do we do it?

Trendelenburg took for his guide in answering this question the Aristotelian principle that like is known by like. Thought is an *active* principle. Therefore, the search must be for an active principle inherent also in being, for being is known by thought. Here Trendelenburg again hypothesized, and—supported by another of Aristotle's principles, "he who knows not motion, knows not nature"—ventured that this primal principle essential to both thought and being might be motion. He then went on to test his hypothesis by showing that the development of this principle can account for everything we know, that it confirms his suspicion that the forms of space and time (and ultimately the other categories) are both subjectively and objectively necessary and valid, and that "The harmony of the subjective and the objective, the union of thought and being in knowledge, is, in so far, made intelligible."[7]

Morris quoted Trendelenburg's triumphant conclusion: "the chasm does not exist, which in other theories separates the categories of thought and the principles of things, as though they belonged to two worlds, which it is impossible to bring into relation, for in their origin all are one."[8] Trendelenburg went still further along this comforting road. He saw nature dominated by the principle of organic operation, in which parts seem to have significance only in relation to the whole and in which all manner of natural phenomena apparently seek to achieve ends. What we have learned scientifically of the operation of efficient causes in the natural world has as yet in no wise accounted for this organic principle; efficient causes can account for things acting but not for things acting toward an end, and so a mechanistic world view is an inadequate one. Our observations of natural phenomena force us to assume that a principle of finality is at work in the natural world, a principle analogous to the characteristic spiritual activity of men by which they project ideal ends and then act to attain them through physical means. Obviously, this assertion that an ideal principle, that thought (or Thought) operates throughout the world of nature, is the crucial step in formulating a natural theology. Again, where Kant had granted that it is impossible to argue to the existence of God from the empirical world and had instead resorted to his postulates of practical reason, Trendelenburg had shown Morris a way to heal the split. The organic operation of the natural world argues to the existence of a guiding intelligence.

A nature that evidenced God: it would seem that Trendelenburg had shown Morris a philosophy that might resolve his crisis of faith. Unhappily, Morris could not accept it. Eventually, in 1873, about the time he wrote the article about Trendelenburg, Morris did achieve a solution of sorts to his problems of faith: he joined the Episcopal Church. But he seems to have won through to faith only at the cost of abandoning the natural. The whole tone of his philosophy in the mid- and late 1870s indicated that he had betaken himself to the security of the transempirical. "True works of art," he wrote in 1876 in an essay criticizing various attempts at formulating a naturalistic aesthetic (Taine's, etc.),

are inspired from above, and not from below; from the more exalted, true life which man leads (whether always consciously or unconsciously) in the realm of real spiritual being, in alliance with the everlasting forms of true being, in direct relation with the Father of all spirits, and not from the lower life and consciousness which are forced upon us from our association with the finite, imperfect scenes of everyday life, and which are therefore not of our making, and hence not truly ours—not a part of ourselves. [9]

In another essay published in 1876, "The Immortality of the

Soul," he showed the same alienation in a remarkable image:

> The water-spider provides for its respiration and life beneath
> the surface of the water by spinning around itself an envelope
> large enough to contain the air it needs. So we have need,
> while walking through the thick and often polluted moral
> atmosphere of this lower world, where seeming life is too fre-
> quently inward death, to maintain around ourselves the purer
> atmosphere of a higher faith. [10]

In Trendelenburg's philosophy, on the other hand, asphyxiation
had threatened from the opposite direction: "thought is suffo-
cated and withers without the air and light of the sensible
cognition of the world of real things and the creative aid of the
imagination, which works with material derived from such
cognition." "Even the most immaterial conceptions, as God,
truth, are realized, if at all, only in direct (positive and negative)
relation to sensible intuition and imagination and their products."[11] But Morris could not now see the natural as an avenue to
the divine; he had withdrawn into the most exaggerated dualism.

∞

As far as his formal philosophy was concerned also, the years
from 1875 to 1878 were Morris's nadir. What original philosophy
he wrote (as distinguished from his work on his translation of
Überweg's history of philosophy) was largely devoted to refutations of materialism and scientism. Its formal approach was still
Trendelenburg's Aristotelianism, but it reads like a lifeless copy of
that doctrine. It wasn't merely that a chilling Manichaeanism
had crept into the Aristotelian framework (where Trendelenburg, for one, would have insisted it didn't belong). This was part
of it, but there was also a narrowness of subject and often an
oppressively defensive tone. Trendelenburg, as Morris portrayed
him, had had a genuine interest in empirical inquiry into the
world of nature. Morris now couldn't have cared less. His only
interest in this regard was in keeping the philosophers and
popularizers of science from overreaching themselves and usurp-
ing the place of speculative philosophers as interpreters of nature
and human experience. If the world evinces any order, purpose-
fulness, or beauty, it cannot be accounted for mechanistically; it

must be "the expression of ideas," of thought controlling "the action of matter." The trouble was that once Morris had said this, he seemed to have nothing more to say. The view of the world he was interested in defending reduced to two or three theological or philosophical propositions (the world is the product of intelligence, etc.); those once said, there was nothing left to do but to reiterate them and stand by them.

How had he come to this position? Why did the philosophy that had made for a lifetime of speculative activity for Trendelenburg become in Morris's case only a "point of view" that he would sporadically reiterate? There seem to have been several reasons. On the one hand, there was the simple fact that he wasn't existing as a philosopher. It was not only that he could not get to teach his subject during his first years at Michigan but that he had trouble finding any sort of philosophical medium or public at all. In 1875 and 1876, for instance, Morris published two articles in the *Journal of the Transactions of the Victoria Institute, or Philosophical Society of Great Britain*.[12] Morris's efforts, even if they were essays in Christian apologetics, were nevertheless serious technical philosophy, but "The Philosophical Society of Great Britain," it turned out, was merely a group of gentlemen and clergymen who felt that the basic truths of Christianity (construed conservatively) ought not to be lost sight of in the face of modern science. They had nothing at all to do with any of the mainstreams of British thought. That Morris's groping for someone to talk to had brought him—knowingly or not—to the "Society" was a pathetic revelation of how lost he was as a philosopher. (Robert Mark Wenley, Morris's biographer, reasoned that Morris *was* aware of the nature of the group and that his trafficking with them was one of the more exaggerated symptoms of his "rebound from skepticism." Either way, it comes to the same thing.) In Germany, studying at the universities with men like Trendelenburg and Ulrici, Morris had been exposed (again, it would be difficult to say how aware of it he was) to philosophy in a professional setting, in which there were organs and facilities for formal dialogue among philosophers and in which the rationale for the pursuit of philosophy was that it is a progressive search for truth, a "science" by which a man or a group of men inquire and criticize, refine methods and correct old mistakes, and advance away from an earlier, grosser ignorance. The adoption of such an ethic may have been a personal impossibility for Morris from the outset; the religious anguish that he was suffering during his entry into philosophy at Union Theological Seminary and then in Germany may have made it certain that he would always be preoccupied with the philosophical evidences for Christianity and that he would have been an apologist no matter what his ambiance in the 1870s. If it was not inevitable, though, what Morris would have needed to keep this professional ethic alive in himself while he was at Michigan was some "countercommunity" to which he might have turned—a group of people and an institution to justify and support his aspirations. Put more concretely, Morris needed an American university world where professional philosophy had a place. But this was not to be had. In the early 1870s there existed no alternate locale for Morris and men like him. He was trapped for the time being in the New England college town of Ann Arbor, Michigan, and he took on the coloration of his environment.

∽

Toward the end of the 1870s George Sylvester Morris's situation was changed dramatically by two events. One was an invitation from the president of the Johns Hopkins University to give some lectures there on a regular basis—of which more later. The other was his happening upon the writings of the British neo-Hegelians, particularly the work of Thomas Hill Green. Green had first distinguished himself by publishing in 1874 a devastating and influential criticism of Hume, and he followed it in 1877 with a similar criticism of Spencer and Lewes. [13] Morris can hardly have begun reading Green much before 1880, yet within a year or two he had adopted Green's philosophy almost whole. Between 1882 and 1889, when he died, Morris, who had not written a book in the twelve or thirteen years since his return from Europe, wrote four of them. [14]

Green's philosophizing makes for complex and often very tortuous reading, yet so far as the speculative side of it is concerned (as distinguished, that is, from the ethical or practical), it can be reduced to two or three central statements. More to the point, we have evidence, direct and indirect, that it was

these few doctrines that drew Morris so quickly to it. John
Dewey, who was introduced to Green by Morris and who as
student, colleague, and personal friend of Morris studied Green
with him for five years, afterward wrote a long essay describing
what he (and, certainly, Morris) had seen in the Englishman's
philosophy. [15] As important as this neo-Hegelianism was to
Morris, it was no less so to young Dewey; under Morris's
influence it was the philosophy that he first adopted as his own
and then gradually transformed into instrumentalism.

T. H. Green was convinced that the theory of knowledge, of
the human soul, and of the nature of the universe put forward
originally by Hume and in modern times notably by Spencer
and Lewes was false. But he had the key strategic insight that
there was only one way in which the modern intellectual world
could be convinced of this, and that was to show that this
philosophy that was being presented as the ally, as the very voice
of modern science, was in reality totally inimical to science, so
inimical that its theory about human knowledge would make
science impossible.

Science, Green said, as an orderly body of knowledge, must
depend on relations; otherwise, the discrete data that it pretends
to order would remain so many utterly isolated facts, completely
unrelated to one another—a chaos. Yet the sensationalism or
empiricism that presents itself as (and is generally considered to
be) the companion philosophy of empirical science is unable to
accommodate this most basic principle. Hume's (and Spencer's)
philosophy, that is to say, holds that the mind is passive and that
all that is in it has come from sensations. If, Green asked, the
relations upon which science depends for its existence are products of sensations, how can they be used to order sensations? If
relations are created by sensations and are used to order sensations, what was it that ordered the original sensations so they
could create those first relations? Other, earlier sensations?
If so, what ordered them?—and so on. Dewey, when he
wanted to illustrate the force of the argument, used Green's
example: "It is," he said, "as if a geologist were to teach that the
first formation of rocks was the product of all layers built upon it,
or as if a physiologist were to teach that a certain digestive act,
exercised by some organism, was the cause of that organism." [16]
It follows, then, that science is not created solely from experi-

ences; rather, science is primarily dependent on the a priori action of intelligence exercising an ordering or relating power which is prior to experience and independent of it—"a spiritual principle."

Kant, of course, had taken the argument essentially this far, and it was Green's next steps that marked him as a Hegelian. He asked how it is that we can say that some experiences are real and others are illusions. It can't be that we test them against "objective reality," meaning the external world, because that— phrased accurately—would be only a matter of testing them against other experiences that are themselves open to the same doubts as to their reality or unreality.

> The external world, therefore, fails us as a criterion. Yet, the fact remains that we *do* decide, successfully, that some experiences are true and others false. If there is no standard *external* to experience by which we do this, it must be by experience itself; it must be that we decide some experiences are illusory because they do not jibe with the rest of our experience. This implies, according to Green, that the world (or a synonym, *the totality of experience*—for that is the only conceivable world there is) is a single, permanent, and all-inclusive system of relations. [17]

This system is the ultimate standard for testing any individual experience. And implied in the existence of this system is the existence of "a permanent single consciousness which forms the bond of relations—'an external intelligence realized in the facts of the world.' " [18]

Thus, in brief, Green arrived at his theistic objective idealism, his neo-Hegelianism. The universe is a system of intelligible relations, but such a system can be only a mental or ideal existence (relations and intelligibility exist only in the mind); therefore the universe exists in no other way than in Mind. As for our finite, distinctively human knowledge of the universe, that is a matter of the Universal Mind partially reproducing itself in our minds under the conditions of time and space.

What drew George Sylvester Morris to this is plain. It did what he wanted done—it asserted the primacy of religion and constructive philosophy over science and scientism—and it did it in a way that was not only philosophically but even rhetorically far superior to anything he knew or had used. Its approach was utterly, disarmingly, positive. Where Morris by 1876 had come to be invariably defensive when the subject of science arose, Green could hail it in the warmest of terms. As Dewey noted a decade or so later, in 1889, Green did not concern himself with the limited, apologetic approach of merely "showing that the main doctrines of theology find no contradiction in the general theories of science," which is a tack Morris had had to take. Instead, the English philosopher went beyond and demonstrated that religion and science "have a common source and a common guaranty," that Hume's and Spencer's associationist philosophies are as destructive to science as they are to religion:

> It was the main work of Green's speculative philosophy to show that there is a spiritual principle at the root of ordinary experience and science, as well as at the basis of ethics and religion; to show, negatively, that whatever weakens the supremacy and primacy of the spiritual principle makes science impossible, and, positively, to show that any fair analysis of the conditions of science will show certain ideas, principles, or categories—call them what you will—that are not physical and sensible, but intellectual and metaphysical.[19]

This was the basic speculative superiority of Green's philosophy that won Morris over. What predominated in Morris's actual writings in the 1880s, however, was another side of Green's Hegelianism—a side that made a really dramatic change in the content and whole tone of Morris's philosophizing.

As we have seen, Morris in the mid-1870s was in danger of ceasing to be a philosopher in any full sense and of becoming an apologist for a small handful of truths that, when the occasion called for it, he would redemonstrate (or, more modestly yet, announce to be still unrefuted). Part of the trouble was that he was compromised by his commitments to religious orthodoxy, but part of it also, very clearly, was that he was at a loss for a certain type of philosophic method. That is to say, once he had asserted that man has a soul and nature a design, he had no idea what more there was to be said about them that had any philosophic import. Nor did he know how to go about making man and nature subjects for further philosophizing. This lack was very likely the purely intellectual content (as distinguished from the temperamental or situational) behind his shrinking from "the finite, imperfect scenes of everyday life." As a matter of fact, it is quite plain from his writings of the seventies that he had given over what he liked to call "the world of the phenomenal" to the scientists, as being the only ones who had a method for dealing with it, and that much of his defensiveness was born of his uneasy half-awareness that most of the intellectual activity of his time was occurring under the aegis of science. He was therefore in the predicament of having to say of that vast endeavor that it was the science of the phenomenal and "not to be confounded with the science of the truly real, or of the true cause, the underlying truth of the real." His voice must have sounded very thin and weak even to himself.

The discovery of Green's Hegelianism changed all that. The logic of Hegel is long and complicated; suffice it to say that it seeks to establish two truths that made all the difference to Morris: that mind and nature are not independent of each other but have an organic relation in that they have a common ground—"spirit"; and that nature (or, the same thing, the Idea of nature) is a phase in the "self-realization of Mind." Morris indicated what this meant for him in a passage at the end of a book he published in 1887, *Hegel's Philosophy of the State and of History*. He was talking about the characteristics of thought:

> Moreover, it is the peculiarity of thought that its objects, its subject-matter, are not away from it, but absolutely present to it and in it. The presumption of thought is, that all its possible objects lie within and not without its own realm, or within the sphere—to employ a truthful figure—of the rational self of the thinker. Thought may therefore fitly be described as the development or realization of the rational self-consciousness of the thinker. Or, more plainly, thought presupposes that things are thinkable; that it and its objects have a common nature; that a common reason informs and constitutes the thinking subject and the objects of thought; that in truly thinking and knowing things it is just as truly developing and actualizing the potentiality of the subject's own nature, or thinking and knowing itself; and so that wherever it may successfully range, whether in the sensible or in the spiritual world, it is no longer a stranger, but strictly at home, and is free. [20]

"No longer a stranger, but strictly at home": after he encountered Green and Green's Hegel there reappeared in Morris's writing the sunny talk of a natural world friendly to the spirit of man that had characterized the philosophy he had learned from Trendelenburg fifteen years earlier, and there disappeared his plaints about "the thick and polluted moral atmosphere of this lower world." Indeed, Morris's conceptualization of original sin—the Fall of Man and his gradual recovery of his original blessedness—sounds as though it has a bit of autobiography hidden in it: the Fall was an alienation, an oppressive sense on man's part of his isolation from the rest of the universe. The Redemption would be a reversal of that:

> By the steps which must follow, in order that knowledge may be according to its own nature complete, the chasm thus apparently established between man and all objects of his knowledge and will is to be bridged over; he is to know, not only his distinction from all other things and beings, but also his essential connection and union with them. So his self-knowledge is to acquire a positive content, his will a substantial motive, and his conduct a fixed and valid law. [21]

With Hegelianism Morris touched earth again. As he now saw it, man in studying nature was studying a partial manifestation of God's nature and, insofar as man also is spiritual, his own nature:

> So, in thinking the thought of nature, in knowing or acquiring knowledge of nature, man can and must assume toward her the attitude of the little child, allowing, or, by experiment, forcing, her to speak for herself . . . and so, *pro tanto*, acquiring spiritual substance—nay, paradoxical as this may seem, developing his own spiritual substance—by inviting and compelling nature to share her own with him. [22]

"Man needs nature and history for self-knowledge and self-realization." In the matter of history, the same results followed: the study of human history became for Morris, as it had for Hegel, the study of the phasic realization of the idea of human freedom through the centuries.

Hegelianism, then, gave Morris a philosophical method and rehabilitated him as a philosopher. It provided him with a way of having the fruits of empiricism, its sure contact with the given world, without having to become a scientist and, more to the point, without having to chance arriving at the conclusion of the empiricist philosophers (Kant included) that the phenomenal world does not evidence God. This method was what Morris called "Real Logic." What he was talking about, of course, was Hegel's logic, whereby the German philosopher discussed all the major eras of history and activities of mankind as steps in the realization of "Absolute Self-Consciousness," man's realization of God, his own spiritual nature, and the true underlying substance of phenomenal reality: the progressive solution, that is to say, of all the problems of philosophy. Now Morris could face the scientists with a method of his own:

> Every instrument . . . intelligently constructed, is constructed
> with reference to an end. The end determines the form of the
> means. In the present case the end is the science of objective
> truth and substantial reality, and the nature of truth and
> reality must determine the method of the science of our quest.
> "A method," says Trendelenburg, "which, as a form, does not
> at the same time grow up out of a profound apprehension
> of the nature of the content, is empty." . . . In like manner,
> Hegel calls the method of philosophy, "not an external form,
> but the very soul and notion of the content" or subject-
> matter. [23]

This method, the development of the Hegelian phenomenology, in which the whole of science and history is shown to be the fulfillment of what is in effect a divine plan, satisfied Morris, no doubt; but to the non-Hegelian it could appear like only a more elaborate and sophisticated apologetic—that behind it was not a disinterested hunger for the truth about nature and man, open to whatever conclusion the facts might dictate, but simply that old drive to justify orthodoxy by whatever means came to hand.

The discovery of Hegelianism was one major event in George Sylvester Morris's life at the end of the 1870s; the other occurred in late 1877, when the Johns Hopkins University invited him to begin an annual series of public lectures in philosophy. Daniel Coit Gilman, the president of the new university, had declared his intention to model it after the great Continental universities, and Morris must have sensed in his offer the opening, at long last, for a recognizable, German-style academic career in philosophy. Content for the moment to divide his time between Johns Hopkins and Michigan (where he was now getting to teach some philosophy), Morris immediately and joyfully accepted the offer. [24]

President Gilman apparently had implied to Morris at the time of his invitation that he would shortly be made the first incumbent of the university's chair of philosophy, and Morris went to Hopkins with that expectation. It was not to be fulfilled. Morris spent his first five years at Hopkins watching the position elude him and, probably, slowly coming to the realization that it would never be his; for, just as a decade earlier Morris's imagination had been caught by the German universities' departments of philosophy, Gilman too had found his ideal in a German university institution. In Gilman's case, however, it was not deductive philosophy but rather research in the physical, social, and historical sciences, and Gilman was inclined to give the chair to an inductionist. Ironically, he may have thought he had one in Morris. Morris's translation in 1872–73 of Überweg's *History of Philosophy* still ranked at the close of the decade as one of the largest endeavors in pure scholarship yet undertaken by an American philosopher, and Morris's subsequent writings in the 1870s were so few and scattered that Gilman may very well have had no idea of what Morris's personal philosophical development had been. Gilman probably considered Morris simply a fine scholar in the history of philosophy, a man who would research and write in that area and encourage his graduate students to do likewise, a man, in short, who participated in the tacit understanding that in university life "production" was the criterion. What Gilman got instead was a man who in his own mind was instructing his audience in the Truth.

Robert Mark Wenley, Morris's biographer and himself another much-abused American idealist philosopher, afterward remarked bitterly that Gilman and too many others had been seduced by the mere tangibility of experimental results and their specious objectivity into confusing data with knowledge. This may have been true, but Gilman was not completely confused. Data, after all, do have something to do with knowledge, even in philosophy. Experimental psychology, to pick the most obvious instance, promised to have something to say about philosophical problems, to take them off the dead center where centuries of speculative disputation had left them. Is man endowed with innate ideas? What is the nature of perception? Science looked as though it might at last begin to settle such questions. And so, in 1882, during Morris's fifth year as a part-time lecturer at Hopkins,

President Gilman hired on G. Stanley Hall, experimental psychologist and scientific pedagogue, fresh back from Germany. Within two years the chair of philosophy was given to Hall, Gilman had his scientist, and Hall commenced to set up his laboratories.

The lives of G. S. Morris and G. Stanley Hall seem to have been planned so as to set in bold relief their eventual meeting at Johns Hopkins in the early 1880s and to give an unobstructed view of the moral to be drawn from that meeting. The first thirty years of the two men's lives were remarkably coincident with each other. Hall, like Morris, was a Vermonter, born in 1844, four years after Morris, in the town of Ashfield. Hall's description of his father could almost have been a portrait of Morris's:

> He was a born fighter, a passionate abolitionist, made war speeches at prayer meetings and in public, imploring the blessing of Heaven upon Lincoln and the northern army, refused to meet a slaveholder who spent his summers in Ashfield, and later grew almost bitter toward Lincoln because he so long delayed to free the slaves and finally did so only as a war measure. [25]

This evangelical upbringing was ratified in Hall's schooling at Williston Academy and at Williams College. Graduating in 1867, he went on to Union Theological Seminary, as had Morris three years earlier. But, where Morris had passed his year at Union in serious study of theology with Professor Henry Boynton Smith, Hall spent his time experiencing the big city and, tutored by Henry Ward Beecher and the godlessness of his Pilgrim Church, unlearning what was being taught him at Union. At the end of his second year in New York, Hall's ambitiousness, Beecher's remarkable responsiveness to this trait, and the purse of a wealthy member of Pilgrim Church combined to pluck him out of Union and put him on board a steamer, bound for Germany. There, as had Morris, he went to Berlin and studied with Trendelenburg and other philosophers and theologians. Hall, however, unlike Morris, also did a little work in physiology, psychology, and medicine. Within the year, however, Hall's money ran out. He came home and "passed through a period of acute discouragement" reminiscent of Morris's: he was deeply in debt, and the president of "a large midwestern state university," suspecting Hall of philosophical and theological relativism, reneged on his promise of a position.[26] Hall was reduced to teaching, unsuccessfully, for brief periods at two New York boys' academies. It was none other than George Sylvester Morris who finally came to his aid by having Hall appointed his successor as tutor for the Seligman children when he himself left for the University of Michigan in 1870.

Hall spent two years in this position before he, too, was appointed to a teaching position at a western college, Antioch in this case. Hall found that his chair, like Morris's at Michigan, was at first "a whole settee, embracing English, French, and German language and literature." Antioch, however, was Unitarian and free; Hall was not discomforted by any orthodoxy during his stay there, and he gradually got to teach more and more philosophy courses. He even managed to make it the three hundred and fifty miles down to Saint Louis, where he talked with William Torrey Harris and the little group who had gathered around him, the "Saint Louis Hegelians."

Hall's actual work—college teaching at Antioch—left him unfulfilled. As he remembered it fifty years later in his auto-biography, this time the way out was shown him by his reading of the recently published first volume of Wilhelm Wundt's *Physiological Psychology*, the book that is generally credited with establishing experimental psychology as an independent science. It was at this point that the parallel between Hall's life and Morris's ended.

Hall left Antioch and, he wrote, "started off for Europe and Wundt." It wasn't quite that simple. He would have taken a position at Johns Hopkins had he been able to convince President Gilman to hire him. Failing that, he went to Harvard and spent two years doing a doctorate in psychology under William James in the Harvard philosophy department. It was the first doctorate ever given by that department and the first in psychology in the United States. Rescued now once and for all from deduction, Hall had established himself as an experimentalist; but outside of Harvard and Johns Hopkins there were as yet no American universities that might hire a psychologist. Voicing a prayer that fate never send him "west again" to the world of small colleges, Hall went on to Germany and more psychology; "I found relatively little time for reading, save in connection with my subject, the physiology of the muscles, on which I focused as I had never done on any subject before."[27] As his second European stay drew to a close, Hall again considered the institutional limitations of the American scene and "finally decided that neither psychology nor philosophy would ever make bread and that the most promising line of work would be to study the applications of psychology to education."[28] So that he might reasonably present himself as an "education psychologist" when he went home, Hall spent his last few months in Europe visiting schools. He then returned to America, set himself up in a small flat in North Somerville, a suburb of Boston, did some lecturing at Williams College, "and waited, and hoped, and worked." One day President Eliot of Harvard "rapped on the door without dismounting from his horse, and asked me to begin Saturday of that week a course of lectures on education."[29] Hall was launched. He lectured that year at Harvard, and in January of the following year, 1882, he gave his first lectures at Hopkins.

This, then, was the man who moved past Morris into the chair at Gilman's university. Up to the point of Hall's decision to leave his college-teaching position at Antioch and to go back to Germany to become an experimental psychologist, the two men's lives are utterly similar in outline. And it is in the light of that same all-important decision that the difference in content becomes so apparent: in the critical, career-making years of his twenties and thirties, Hall was proof against the pieties that immobilized George Sylvester Morris. The difference is there to be seen in Hall's quick gravitation in 1867 toward Henry Ward Beecher's congregation of *arrivistes* and later in his long-distance cultivation of the Saint Louis administrator-intellectuals, the "Hegelians." It is there, too, at another level in his impious detachment from what was being preached at Union Theological by the Henry Boynton Smiths and, the following year, in the coolness with which he watched the giants of German philosophy and theology parade before him—a coolness apparent in his ironic distance from their doctrines and his valet's eye for the comical details of their personal and professional lives.[30] The impression in all these scenes is of the young man traveling light, not risking any encumbering baggage of filiopiety or other such commitments as Morris carried. And in the end it was Hall who possessed the simplicity of impulse, the uncluttered, uncomplicated ambitiousness, that made it possible for the young man to prevail.

3   Dewey at Hopkins

President Gilman would have been irritated had he understood how easy a transition it was for young Dewey to leave the provincial-college culture of Burlington, Vermont, and come to Gilman's graduate school. The trouble, as Gilman would have seen it, was that Dewey immediately encountered the least-professional thing in his German-style professional school, the classrooms of George Sylvester Morris.

The arrangement in the Hopkins philosophy department during the two years that Dewey was a student there was that Morris would be in residence and teaching in the fall semester while Hall was away; then, in the second semester, Morris would go off to Michigan and Hall would teach his psychology courses. The practical effect of this in Dewey's case was that in his first semester at Hopkins he took three courses from Morris, "The Science of Knowledge" (a seminar in epistemology), "History of Philosophy in Great Britain" (a four-hour-a-week lecture course devoted, to judge from Morris's book *British Thought and Thinkers*, to an explication and idealist criticism of British sensationalist philosophy), and a lecture course, "Hegel's Philosophy of History."[1]

It could have been predicted that this would be a fatal dose of idealist philosophy for Dewey, and so it was: by the end of the semester he had thoroughly absorbed Morris's philosophical outlook. In December of that first semester he delivered a paper to the University Metaphysical Club entitled "Knowledge and the Relativity of Feeling," which argued that the pet sensationalist doctrine that our feelings (or sensations) are relative actually implies that we *do* have an objective knowledge of reality, for it is only with reference to some objective criterion that we can call anything relative. As Dewey noted when he offered the address to Harris for publication in the *Journal of Speculative Philosophy*, this was "the same kind of argument" he had used to refute materialism in the first article he had written for Harris two years earlier. The difference was that in that first effort he had set out to prove only that materialism cannot logically be asserted; now, after his semester with Morris, he had a more ambitious goal: to imply the existence, and our knowledge, of the Universal Mind. [2]

This advance of Dewey's is a convenient symbol of the nature of his transfer from Torrey's tutelage to Morris's and of the ease with which it occurred. In Torrey, Dewey had seen a fragmented defense of orthodoxy—part philosophy, part faith, part "reserved judgment"; in Morris (thanks to Green and the neo-Hegelians) he encountered essentially the same orthodoxy championed by a breathtakingly grandiose system, one that met the empiricists and skeptics on their own grounds and outlogicked them. More: where Torrey had been hard put to it to maintain theism as at least a reasonable possibility, the Hegelianism Dewey learned in Morris's classrooms established it as a necessity. [3] In his auto-biographical essay many years later, Dewey attributed his conversion to Hegelianism in part to its satisfaction of an "intense emotional craving" on his part to overcome the "dualisms" in New England culture. [4] But Dewey had a habit of crediting his younger selves with insights and convictions that they did not in fact possess, and he may have been doing it here, too; certainly he, like Morris, had solid intellectual reasons for "going Hegelian," and, in Morris, Dewey was again encountering the type of figure he was so likely to become a disciple of. [5] Thanks largely to this particular reminiscence of Dewey's and to the antidualist philosophy for which he is remembered, the tendency has been to see his embracing of Hegelian monism as a sharp change in his intellectual directions, a "repudiation of Vermont" or some such thing. Actually it was anything but that: his former teacher Torrey's objections to Hegel's objective idealism had been that he thought it issued in a pantheism that went counter to orthodoxy and that it tended to submerge the individual personality and will. Green's and Morris's (and now Dewey's) neo-Hegelianism was at great pains to establish that it did nothing of the sort. [6] Dewey became a Hegelian because it was the best philosophy he had yet seen, because Morris's version of it had the same objectives as Torrey's mixture of intuitionalism and Kantianism, and because of its immediate association in those first months in

Baltimore with Morris and with what young Dewey took to be the spirit and milieu of the university.

By the end of his first semester at Johns Hopkins, Dewey, what with his presence in all of Morris's courses, his presentation of "Knowledge and the Relativity of Feeling" before the Metaphysical Club, and his being the only student majoring in the history of philosophy (Morris's special purview in the department), had established himself in Morris's eyes as his prize pupil. Accordingly, Morris had Dewey appointed to give the undergraduate course in the history of philosophy in the second semester, when he himself would be away at Michigan. The textbook was to be Morris's own translation of Überweg's *History*. In the same letter in which he told Torrey about this honor, Dewey mentioned that he would be taking Hall's courses in psychology during the second semester: "I don't see any very close connection between it and phil. [*sic*] but I suppose it will furnish grist for the mill, if nothing else." He also told Torrey that besides attending the lectures in experimental, physiological, and speculative psychology (this last had to do with the philosophical implications of empirical psychology), he was doing some experiments: "one set to determine, if possible, what effect fixing attention upon one thing very strongly, has upon a 'remainder' in consciousness, and the other the effect attention has in producing involuntary muscular movements—something after the 'mind' reading fashion."[7] Dewey gave two public presentations that semester, both of them papers delivered at meetings of the Metaphysical Club. "Hegel and the Theory of the Categories" was one of them; the other was a Hegelian criticism of Kant titled "Kant and Philosophic Method," which was published a year later in the *Journal of Speculative Philosophy*.[8]

The following autumn again found Dewey studying with Morris, this time in a course on the history of German philosophy and a seminar on Spinoza's *Ethics*. More and more he was coming to sound like Morris, taking up his mentor's themes and complaints as quickly as he had absorbed his philosophy the year before. He grumbled about the short shrift given to philosophy at Gilman's university ("No one realizes more than I the great benefits of the [philosophy] courses given here, but no one realizes more than the instructors I presume their inadequacy to cover the ground which a University ought to cover"),[9] and he was quietly scandalized at the runaway empiricism that marked the university's offerings in other areas. At the beginning of his fourth and last semester at Hopkins he wrote to Harris:

> I am taking as a minor subject the theory of state, international law, etc., in the historical department, and am in pretty close contact with the men there. It is the largest, and in the character of its students about the strongest department in the University, but there is no provision to give them the philo-sophic side of their own subjects. The philosophy of history and of social ethics is untouched, and as long as it remains so, they don't get more than half the good of their own courses it seems to me. [10]

By "the philosophy of history" Dewey meant what Morris meant when he wagged his finger at the researchers:

> History is the example, *plus* that which it exemplifies. It is the example, *plus* its teaching. It is the "fact" seen in the relations which alone render it comprehensible. . . . It is, in short, the fact seen as the illustration and phenomenal incarnation of a universal and livingly operative reason, Logos, or logic, which, interior to the fact, is the ground of its reality, and, transcend-ing the particular fact, connects it with all other facts, and so is the ground of its intelligibility. [11]

It was Hegel's philosophy of history, and philosophy itself as the queen of the university disciplines, taking precedence over the various empiricisms and giving them their meaning. "I hope that when the public mind is somewhat at rest on the subject of 'sciences' in education," Dewey closed primly, "there may be a humble agitation in favor of smuggling philosophy in some-where; and that it will be found not altogether absurd to urge that our theology, our politics, and possibly even our science itself would be none the worse for thorough and scientific treatment of philosophy in our universities and colleges." [12]

In this third semester at Johns Hopkins, Dewey, having decided to try to complete his graduate studies that year, set to work on a dissertation. For a topic he chose to develop the paper on "Kant and Philosophic Method" that he had written the previous spring. His dissertation would be about Kant's "psy-chology,"

> . . . that is, his psychology of spirit (so far as he has any) or

the subjective side of his theory of knowledge, in which besides giving a general acc't. of his theory of Sense, Imagination, etc., I hope to be able to point out that he had the conception of Reason or Spirit as the center and organic unity of the entire sphere of man's experience, and that in so far as he is true to this conception that he is the true founder of modern philo- sophic method, but that in so far as he was false to it he fell into his own defects, contradictions, etc. [which Hegel then resolved]. [13]

Dewey's dissertation, then, was very much in keeping with the rest of his graduate studies under George Sylvester Morris. There was, however, another side to Dewey's experience and growth at Hopkins, and it was not until his fourth and last semester there that it really took voice.

ထ

In the autobiographical sketch he wrote when he was seventy years old, Dewey recalled the prevalence of Scottish common- sense philosophy in the 1870s and 1880s and the "almost sacrosanct air that enveloped the idea of 'intuitions.' " "Some- how," he remembered, "the cause of all holy and valuable things was supposed to stand or fall with the validity of intuition- alism."[14] Dewey neglected to mention that he himself had had a brush with intuitionalism, that he had used it as a temporary solution to his own personal philosophical problems, and—most surprisingly—that it was even *after* his exposure to the more advanced and sophisticated Hegelianism at Johns Hopkins that he had turned to it.

In early March 1884, his second and last year at Hopkins, Dewey read a paper entitled "The New Psychology" before the university's Metaphysical Club. Printed later that year in the *Andover Review*, it became Dewey's fifth publication and the first to appear outside the *Journal of Speculative Philosophy*. [15] It is generally recognized as a turning point in his thinking, his initial essay on experimental psychology, and the herald of what was to be a lifelong interest in that science.

Dewey's essay was in the form of a greeting to the New Psychology. The old science of the mind, he said, was dominated by abstractions and schemata utterly inadequate to "the infinite detail and complexity of the simplest psychical life, its inter-weavings with the physical organism, with the life of others in the social system." But now we have a psychology that, thanks to the spirit of the age—sated with system and longing for fact—and to the new tool, experimentation, goes beyond the old categories. Its progress has been enriched by concepts drawn from biology (concepts such as organism and environment) and from the new social and historical sciences. We may expect great things from it.

Unlike the previous four articles, which were clear, closely reasoned, and easily followed, this essay had the breathless, difficult tone that usually signaled one of Dewey's epiphanies. It is probably the pervasive excitement of the article that has led Dewey's commentators to overlook the fact that its last two pages, in which Dewey outlined the rewards the New Psychology would bring, are as obscure as any he ever wrote, denser by far than the rest of the article, and, with no more context than Dewey gave, incomprehensible. "The New Psychology," Dewey wrote, "would not have necessary truths about principles; it would have the touch of reality in the life of the soul. It rejects formalistic intuitionalism for one which has been well termed dynamic. It believes that truth, that reality, not necessary *beliefs about* reality, is given in the living experience of the soul's development." He went on:

> It emphasizes the teleological element, not in any mechanical or external sense, but regarding life as an organism in which immanent ideas or purposes are realizing themselves through the development of experience. Thus modern psychology is intensely ethical in its tendencies. As it refuses to hypostatize abstractions into self-subsistent individuals, and as it insists upon the automatic spontaneous elements in man's life, it is making possible for the first time an adequate psychology of man's religious nature and experience. . . . It finds no insuper-able problems in the relations of faith and reason, for it can discover in its investigations no reason which is not based upon faith, and no faith which is not rational in its origin and ten-dency. But to attempt to give any detailed account of these features of the New Psychology would be to go over much of the recent discussion of ethics and theology. We can conclude only by saying that following the logic of life, it attempts to comprehend life. [16]

Dewey's source here was a small body of work by an American Protestant theologian, at this time the pastor of the First Congregational Church in New Haven, Newman Smyth. Several of the key phrases in Dewey's peroration seem almost certainly to have come from Smyth: "reality, not necessary *beliefs about* reality, . . . given in the living experience of the soul's development," "life . . . an organism in which immanent ideas or purposes are realizing themselves through the development of experience," and the term "dynamic intuitionalism." The other ideas and lines of argument in the article could have had a variety of sources; but when it is read against the works in which Smyth developed his position, it is clear that much of Dewey's article, "The New Psychology," drew its inspiration from Smyth. [17]

Newman Smyth was born in 1843 in Brunswick, Maine, where his father was a professor at Bowdoin. Smyth himself went to Bowdoin, graduating in 1863. A few months later he enlisted in the Sixteenth Maine Volunteers, was soon made an officer, and saw combat in Virginia, outside Petersburg. At the end of the war he went to Andover Theological Seminary to train for the ministry. The theological liberalism for which Andover was later distinguished was not yet dominant there, and Smyth found it still something of a stronghold of the "New England theology." Probably the only bitter words Smyth ever wrote about another man were in his memories of its principal exponent at Andover, Professor Edward Park; he condemned him for his desiccated theological rationalism, his regiments of biblical "proof texts," his "complete system of theological definitions and deductions." Upon graduation from the seminary, Smyth, convinced by his experience in the Civil War of the necessity of "repeated contacts with life in the raw," began his ministry at the bottom in a mission chapel near the industrial tenements of Providence, Rhode Island. There he underwent a crisis of faith that he later blamed on the abstract lifelessness of the theology he had been taught by Park. Now, in doubt, he went over to Germany, to Berlin and Halle, just as George Sylvester Morris had done three years earlier, to look for spiritual sustenance and to think things through. He studied with Dorner and Tholuck, two great evangelical theologians of the "mediating school," both disciples of Schleiermacher, and with Ulrici, whom he credited in his first book with being the only man doing enough to bring together

Schleiermacher's account of the origin of faith with "modern scientific theories of man's origin and history."[18]

Smyth found what he was after in Germany, and, his faith reborn, he came back to America the following year. He entered the parish ministry in Quincy, Illinois, and in his spare time began to write about his German experiences. Smyth outlined the position that attracted Dewey so greatly in three small articles: "The Dynamical Theory of the Intuitions," in the 1878 volume of the *New Englander*; "Orthodox Rationalism," in the 1882 *Princeton Review*; and "Professor Harris's Contribution to Theism," in the 1884 *Andover Review*. The first of these articles was a reply to a review of Smyth's first book, *The Religious Feeling*, that was published in an earlier number of the *New Englander* by Samuel Harris, a member of the Andover faculty when Smyth was a student there. The last of the three articles was Smyth's review of a book by Harris. Smyth saw Harris as a very advanced and enlightened propounder of the New England theology, an exponent of a purportedly up-to-date Scottish common-sense realism, and it was largely in the form of a criticism of Harris's doctrine that Smyth outlined his "dynamic" intuitionalism. [19]

The central argument of Harris's old-style intuitionalism, as Newman Smyth saw it, was that God and the moral and spiritual order *must* exist because man, the way his mind is constituted, must believe them to exist. Smyth had numerous objections to this, stemming from a variety of sources. The first is obvious and needs little explaining: philosophically he found it unconvincing. The movement from the proposition that man must believe that God exists to the proposition that therefore God does exist he thought invalid: it slipped into the conclusion a key element that had not been contained in the premises. [20] Smyth's second objection is a subtler one; he found Harris's reasoning to be a type of what Smyth liked to call "orthodox rationalism." That is, he felt that, in forming their response to Hume, the intuitionalist philosophers had committed the strategic error of meeting him on his own grounds. Unconsciously, they had accepted the world view and theology of the eighteenth-century deists that had issued in Hume's agnosticism: a world of mechanical order inhabited by men whose souls are an orderly collection of discrete faculties, a world that had been made and set going by a watchmaker God and then abandoned to run itself. Smyth believed that the intuitionalists had thus left themselves (and their descendants, such as Harris) trying to prove a Christianity that was not really Christianity at all—a religion without individual providence, without a personal, reciprocal relationship between the individual Christian in prayer and his God, and without any integral connection with the central events of Christian history: the Incarnation and the Redemption. To be sure, they believed and preached these truths; yet when it came to a *philosophical* defense of Christianity, they were trying to prove only a deism. [21]

Smyth's third source of objection to Harris and the philosophy he represented was Smyth's alertness to the development in the German laboratories of physiological psychology. The picture of man, his mind and behavior, that was emerging from these, he felt, was totally at variance with the psychology assumed by the common-sense intuitionalists in their proofs of theism. [22] No evidence was being found for the existence of separate "faculties" or "powers" in the mind; at best, "faculty" might serve as a shorthand term for indicating certain types or aspects of activity, but even here it served poorly a science that was struggling to describe the intricate flow of psychic activity that was revealing itself in experiment—"one continuous living synthesis," Smyth called it. On these three counts, then, Smyth dismissed the "static" intuitionalists as "the constitutional lawyers of human nature," philosophers whose psychology was "atomistic rather than ... organic." [23]

Smyth introduced his counterdoctrine, dynamic intuitionalism, with an inquiry. "Professor Harris," he said,

In common with most theistic writers, holds stoutly to a theory of presentative intuition, and hence real knowledge, so far as the external world presented to our senses is concerned. Theism has to raise and to answer the further question, Whether there is any corresponding presentation, and any consequent reality, in our spiritual consciousness? Do we in any way come into actual contact with, are we living in real relation to, a spiritual as well as a physical environment? Are the persistent spiritual life and the religious consciousness of man an indication of soul-contact with a spiritual and divine Reality in which we have our being? [24]

The substance of dynamic intuitionalism was Smyth's answer

to these questions. First of all, he admitted that he shared with Scottish common-sense intuitionalists their basic premise that man has a religious nature, that a belief in the higher things is natural to human consciousness. And, much as they did, he absolved himself from having to defend his premise, granting that he could not "prove these assertions to be true to any one who denies that he has the reason for faith in his own experience." But, he added, "neither can any man prove to any other man the reality of the world grasped by our senses." We can only affirm that these are the implications of our own individual consciousness and of the general consciousness of humanity. Simply to stop with this fact of man's natural theism, however, and to talk about it as irreducible, as part of the constitution of the human mind, is not enough, Smyth maintained. Rather, following the lead of present-day science and its central findings that all things have evolved and that to view the "constitution" of anything as an ultimate fact is false, we have to inquire into the *genesis* of this natural belief in God. Again like the scientists, we have to posit the hypothesis that seems to answer best and most economically for what we already know about the origins of theism within us and also to promise the most fruitful framework for further research into the question. This hypothesis Smyth found in Schleiermacher's doctrine that just as our knowledge of the physical world and all our empirical science have their origin in sensation, in physical feeling, so do we have an analogous *capacity to feel* in our spiritual nature. Correspondingly, just as the universal human convictions about things having to do with the physical world (say, mathematical axioms or the principles of contradiction and causality) are a true reading of our environment—"not . . . mere forms of thought imposed upon things; but rather the real relations of things imposing themselves upon any intelligence capable of receiving them"—so is mankind's general belief in God a true reading of our *spiritual* environment, an effect of "the immediateness of the Divine presence and working in our thinking, or . . . God's self-revelation through the spiritual and rational life of the world." [25] On both sides, then,

> Our rational consciousness is the inevitable resultant of the powers, natural and spiritual, among which we live, and which are always acting upon us. We are ourselves personally present in the omnipresence of God.

Smyth concluded his presentation of dynamic intuitionalism as follows:

> According to this view of our existence, or personal presence, in God's omnipresence, our religious consciousness and life cannot be explained except as implying the reality of a spiritual environment, any more than man's physical consciousness can be explained without the implication in it of an external physical environment. [26]

∞

To understand why Smyth's suggestion (it was hardly elaborate enough to be called a system) had an impact on Dewey, why so much of the first turning point in his public intellectual life was couched in its language, we must take a look at what we know of Dewey's situation and derive a few of the corollaries of Smyth's philosophy.

Most of what has been written about Dewey has been in effect a chronicle of his creativity, the emphasis being on his great drive and his originality. This is entirely correct as far as it goes; it would be hard to say too much about these qualities in him. But there ought to be a corresponding emphasis on his piety—not so much in the narrow sense of religious faith as in the broader meaning of faithfulness to an upbringing and a culture. The form and quality of his achievement were as much a product of this as of his intellectual boldness and energy. We have seen that his discipleship to Morris—despite what H. A. P. Torrey might have thought of the Hegelianism—was basically in keeping with this New England church culture. Morris was a churchman, and his Hegelianism was decidedly right wing. The use to which he put philosophy—the defense of Christianity and certain related beliefs, free will, the spirituality of the soul—was exactly the use to which Torrey and the common-sense ministers had always put it. This background largely accounts for Dewey's four early publications in the journal of the Saint Louis Hegelians, his logical refutations of materialism, scientism, and relativism, and his demonstration of the superiority of Hegel to Kant. They were all dutiful. The first two were schoolboy exercises (with Torrey as schoolmaster); the latter two could have been written by Morris himself.

During his two years of graduate study at Johns Hopkins, however, a new element had come into Dewey's world. In the spring semester of both years, while Morris was away at Michigan, Dewey had been studying physiological psychology with G. Stanley Hall and had been mightily attracted to it. The laboratory and the seminar were the most glamorous institutions of the new university life in the 1880s, and the activities that accompanied them, experiment and research, were accepted as the sources, par excellence, of new knowledge. Josiah Royce afterward wrote the classic description of the Hopkins scene:

> The "conflict" between "classical" and "scientific" education was henceforth to be without significance for the graduate student. . . . The beginning of the Johns Hopkins University was a dawn wherein " 'twas bliss to be alive." The air was full of rumors of noteworthy work done by the older men of the place, and of hopes that one might find a way to get a little working power one's self. . . . No, the academic life was something much more noble and serious than such "discipline" had been in its time. The University wanted its children to be, if possible, not merely well-informed, but productive. She preached to them the gospel of learning for wisdom's sake, and of acquisition for the sake of fruitfulness. One longed to be a doer of the word, and not a hearer only, a creator of his own infinitesimal fraction of a product, bound in God's name to produce it when the time came. [27]

Plainly, there was something of the eternal (or transcultural, at least) in what Royce described: youths achieving manhood. But it also had another dimension: the disintegration of one very specific culture. The classical college ideal of character formation in which they had been raised was being suddenly supplanted in those few years at Hopkins by a new ideal: science or learning for learning's sake. Instead of fashioning their identities within the forms of a stable subculture, they were, so to speak, participating in the changing of the very forms of manhood itself.

Fifty years later, when John Dewey was collaborating with his daughter on a brief biographical sketch, he referred back to this much-quoted passage from Royce and repeated it: ". . . it was bliss to be alive and in such surroundings." [28] He had forgotten that there was also material here for uneasiness. Dewey was anything but immune to the enormous cultural impact the laboratory was having on his fellow graduate students at Hopkins and to the fact that research was the very embodiment of self-realization for them. George Sylvester Morris, on the other hand, was asking the reverse of his young disciple Dewey: not new discoveries but faithfulness to an old ideal. His classroom, with its lecturing, philosophizing, and preaching, recalled the "Mental and Moral Philosophy" of the pre–Civil War American colleges and seminaries. It was a symbol of stasis, and Hall's winning of the Hopkins chair of philosophy in 1884 and Morris's defeat were symbols of its lack of a future. Dewey was torn between Morris and Hall, between his loyalties and his nascent ambitions.

On a more general plane, Dewey was caught up in the difficulty that was besetting theology and ethics at large. Not just in the new American universities but throughout the culture— thanks to the vogue of Spencer after his grand tour of the country in the 1870s and to such organs of scientism as the *Popular Science Monthly*—spiritual doctrines were suffering the embarrassments of nakedness. It was an age and a public that seemed to have gone mad on science: a bad time for theologies and ethics founded on apriorisms, deductions, and abstract, intricate arguments about "the nature of the soul." Young Dewey was only one of many pious men who were becoming convinced that somehow it would have to be demonstrated that religion is "scientific" too. His situation was particularly difficult because science, for him, was Hall's experimental psychology, and theistic philosophy was Morris's Hegelianism. Bringing the one into a genuinely sustaining relationship with the other looked to be impossible.

The difficulty, which had to do with the logic of Hegelianism itself, is a subtle one, and most of Dewey's intellectual growth over the next several years was to be in the form of an attempted solution of it. The main thrust of Hegelian philosophy is that subject and object, the knower and the known, are not ontologically separate, but that nature exists in and for thought. This is just another way of saying that metaphysics *is* philosophical psychology, "the science of the mind." Plainly, then, for psychology to be both empirical and Hegelian would be a contradiction. So Dewey, in effect, was in a dilemma: if philosophical psychology is indeed an independent area of inquiry, then the world is not objective mind, and psychology can be studied only at the cost of sliding back into the original dualism between mind and matter that the adoption of Hegel's objective idealism had been meant to solve. If, on the other hand, the world *is* objective mind, then there is no psychology, for deductive metaphysics subsumes it.[29]

When Dewey read Smyth's little articles, he may have thought he saw in them a godsend that promised to answer all his problems, to enable him to enter the study of psychology with all his philosophical and evangelical flags flying. To begin with, Smyth appeared to offer a solution to Dewey's dilemma concerning psychology and dualism, for Smyth held *both* to the need for physiological psychology *and* to an objective epistemology. And if his epistemology (and his philosophy at large) was not really a Hegelian one, this lapse was at least in part compensated for by Smyth's insistence that an empirical psychology is not only compatible with epistemological realism but is in fact necessary to it.

Smyth maintained that the way to escape dualism, "the only method by means of which we may hope to overleap the scepticism of Kant, and to gain the high ground above the materialism which is 'the slough of despond' of modern thought," is to "understand mind as a spiritual unity in relation to the forces, physical, moral, spiritual with which it is alive."

> Mind is to . . . [this] view not an instrument but an organism; thought is not in its origin an exercise of reason, but a manifestation of a life. As a plant is not to be conceived of as a collection of cells bound together into a system according to some specific type, but as an organism growing from a hidden root, shaped by various forces, and pulsating with sunbeams; so, and much more significantly, mind is an organic unity, having its hidden root beneath consciousness in the deep things of God, vibrating with manifold influences, and tremulous with the Light in which its life blossoms.

"This philosophy," he continued,

> accepts loyally the first truths, the primitive cognitions, in which the Scotch metaphysics rests; but it regards them as the exponents of the powers which make man what he is; and beneath the first-fruits of rational consciousness it seeks to apprehend the spiritual and divine chemistry of their growth. . . . [It seeks to understand how] man comes to himself in the midst of the powers of the universe, and is in all his manifold,

conscious life himself a pulsating centre of forces, a being of
wonderful receptivities and activities. [30]

What Smyth did here was to provide Dewey with some of the
vision and vocabulary that would dominate his writings on
psychology for years to come. Smyth's proposal, reduced to the
logic of its core, would read something like this: evolutionary
biology has shown us that a plant is to be understood as an
organism that is the product of an evolving interaction between
an original impulse toward (or seed of) life and an environment;
this gives us an explanatory model both for the becoming of this
individual plant and for the long-term becoming of the species of
which it is a member. Similarly, just as this has proved to be the
most profitable way of understanding a plant, so too the most
promising mode for understanding man is *not* to haggle endlessly
over whether he can know reality directly (Hume's and Kant's
question) but rather to view him too as an organism, both natural
and spiritual, the result of a life-impulse and an environment (or
number of environments).

Smyth would append a note to his model by way of reply to the
anticipated criticism from dualist critics that he had not answered
the dualist question, Can man know nature or reality?, but had
instead gone around it. Smyth's response would be, first, that the
dualist question is now a nonquestion because it violates the
canon of procedure that subject and environment (man and the
world) are not to be viewed as being apart, even hypothetically;
and, second, that as a proof that the question is nonsense we have
the fact that it is insoluble—those who try to answer it will be in it
forever, caught in a perpetual prolegomenon, denied all progress.
On the other hand, the scientist, following Smyth's hypothesis,
will have as a sign that his is the proper approach an ever
growing understanding of man through his interaction with his
environment. (Students of Dewey's writings will recognize this
handling of such challenges as one of Dewey's favorite tactics,
also.)

Dewey's dilemma was solved. True, Smyth's epistemology
wasn't quite Hegelian, but it had all the virtues that had originally
recommended Hegelianism to Morris and his young protégé. First,
it granted men an objective knowledge of reality. (It was by way
of drawing attention to this crucial equivalence between Smyth

and Hegel that Dewey insisted, in "The New Psychology," that this psychology "believes that truth, that reality, not necessary *beliefs about* reality, is given in the living experience of the soul's development.") Second, it did for Dewey what Hegelianism did not: it left room for an empirical psychology as a specifically philosophic endeavor. Indeed, it positively demanded it as a way of studying God's progressive revelation to us.

Again, the logic behind Smyth's assertion is simple: if spiritual truths are revealed to us through processes analogous to those by which natural truths come to us,[31] the study of either of the analogous processes sheds light on the other. And so it follows:

> We need for Christian theology a psychology which shall be true to the actual processes of man's life; which shall seek to understand consciousness, not by verbal dissection of it, but by following its living development; which shall have some account to give of the rise of ideas out of impressions [i.e., of the genesis of constitutional ideas from sensations or feelings, both natural and spiritual]; of the crystallization of undefined and general elements of consciousness into conceptions; of the formation of intellectual feelings in Schleiermacher's sense into rational beliefs.[32]

That is why, at the end of his own article "The New Psychology," Dewey trumpeted:

> It emphasizes the teleological element, not in any mechanical or external sense, but regarding life as an organism in which immanent ideas or purposes are realizing themselves through the development of experience. *Thus modern psychology is intensely ethical in its tendencies.*[33]

These happy conclusions were drawn from Smyth's claim that the physical and the spiritual are analogous. But Smyth actually went much further than this, and in so doing he opened another path down which Dewey would walk five years later. As we have said, all of Dewey's conclusions here rest on Smyth's mere claim that the spiritual and the natural, though separate and different planes of existence, are analogous planes. In reality, Smyth was claiming much more. He was convinced that the doctrine that Christ had redeemed the world meant at least that the spiritual and natural were no longer apart but were now ends of the same continuum, and he was even prepared to say that, now, *any* distinction between the divine and the worldly is an artificial one, for they have been united in Christ for all men.

This bold theology had two effects. First, it rendered man's natural environment and experience thoroughly benevolent, a redeemed instrument in God's continuing revelation and providence. It enabled Smyth to say: "Granted these universal rational and spiritual phenomena [i.e., the constitutional beliefs again], this is their significance; they are simply the effect upon us of our total and real environment."[34] The second effect of Smyth's speculation that the Incarnation had universally brought together the divine and the natural was that it did not leave psychology as just an ancillary science to theology—and, in that limited sense, ethical; it actually made psychology the very substance of the theology of God's transaction with mankind. Thus Smyth:

> The truest psychology is that which is based upon the regener ated consciousness of man. That is not an adequate philosophy of human nature which explains only the natural man, and has no comprehension of Jesus' oneness in his perfect humanity with the Father. The more fully man realizes himself in the world, the more purely and perfectly he becomes man, the more confident does he grow of his spiritual birthright, and the reality in the universe of God.[35]

In effect—and what glad news this must have been to Dewey— good science is good theology.

Smyth was aware of the danger that this type of speculation might "leave us in mysticism, or betray us into pantheism," that is, that in coming so close to identifying the spiritual and the worldly we run the risk that the natural may be totally absorbed into the divine. He seems to have forgotten that there was another danger here. The reverse might happen: the divine might become totally absorbed in the natural. We have granted the old-fashioned intuitionalists very little in this study, so perhaps we ought to allow them the last word here. In defending their doctrines against Hegelianism and the like, they used to warn their students that at the end of every venture down the primrose path of idealism there lurked naturalism and a Spinoza—or, we might add, a Dewey.

4   Psychology

Several months after he had delivered "The New Psychology," Dewey received his doctorate from Hopkins. He had no job offer for the fall, and he suffered a bad moment when none came through in the early summer. Finally, in July, he received an invitation from Morris and the University of Michigan to come with the rank of instructor to assist his former mentor in teaching the university's offerings in philosophy and psychology. George H. Howison, another theistic idealist like Morris, who had been his assistant the previous year at Michigan, had just left for the University of California, and so the post was open. It was a good time for Dewey to be going to the University of Michigan. It was entering a period of expansion and professionalization, and Morris was at last about to become head of the philosophy department.

Whether he knew it or not, Morris's hiring of Dewey was a wise move politically. The previous year there had been student objection to the fact that they were receiving an unalloyed dose of idealism from the philosophy department; Morris and Howison, the campus newspaper suggested, might be afraid to expose the students to the empiricist philosophers, to Mill and Spencer and Lewes. Dewey, as Howison's successor, apparently had enough empiricist credentials and interests to quiet the protest. He began to teach a wide variety of courses in psychology ("Empirical Psychology," "Experimental Psychology," "Speculative Psychology," etc.), and several others in philosophy on such topics as Kant's ethics and his *Critique of Pure Reason*, Spencer, and formal logic. Morris handled the rest of the philosophy offerings, teaching courses on the history of philosophy (ancient and modern), and on ethics, aesthetics, and Hegelian logic. [1]

Dewey's empiricist bent should not be allowed to obscure the fact that he was still a theistic idealist himself. He came to

Michigan well recommended as being completely trustworthy in his orthodoxy, and within two months of his arrival he delivered an address to the Student Christian Association which bore out the recommendations. [2] The homily, "The Obligation to Knowledge of God," began:

> The scriptures are uniform in their treatment of scepticism. There is an obligation to know God, and to fail to meet this obligation is not to err intellectually, but to sin morally. Belief is not a privilege, but a duty,—"whatsoever is not of faith is sin." To a generation like ours this is a hard saying. We treat sceptics not as those who have failed to meet a duty, but as unfortunates whose peculiar mental constitution is depriving them of the blessings of God's presence. Many sceptics declare that their greatest sorrow is that they live as orphans in an orphaned world, without the Divine Father, and that their greatest joy would be the knowledge of Him. But the statements of Christ and his immediate followers are explicit. To fail to get knowledge in these matters is not an intellectual, but a moral defect. [3]

This was stern stuff, but, Dewey cautioned the softhearted, the scriptural doctrine has lately been reconfirmed—by modern experimental psychology. It has shown that the intellect, will, and affections are completely interdependent, "that there is no knowledge of anything except as our interests are alive to the matter, and our will actively directed toward the end desired." "We know only what we most *want* to know. ... God is everlastingly about us, and to fail to know Him is to show that we do not wish to know Him." [4]

Dewey's later specifically religious contributions to Michigan publications became much more liberal; had he been confronted with "The Obligation to Knowledge of God" a few years later, it is safe to say that he would have been rather embarrassed. His little sermon, however, with its odd mixture of elements— old-time religion, new psychology, and even some of Morris's philosophy—was not merely a freakish occurrence, for his first semester or so at Michigan appears to have been a time of considerable intellectual confusion for Dewey. That same autumn he delivered an address on "Mental Evolution" to the university's Philosophical Society, and that paper, too, seems to have contained disparate elements. Like so many of Dewey's early unprinted efforts, it has been lost, but a student reporter summarized it in the campus newspaper:

> Mr. Dewey began by showing the inadequacy of the con-
> ception of life as given by the old philosophers, and by
> developing three principles fundamental to and involved in a
> proper and consistent conception of life. He showed that life
> must be looked upon as an organic whole, whose parts are
> interdependent and in close relation; that man's environment
> consists of everything, near and remote, that exists in organic
> relation with him; that mental growth, therefore, in man,
> individually and collectively, is determined by the scope of his
> environment, that is by his universe.
>
> This conception, the Doctor claimed, does away with the
> mechanical and material notions of mind held by the old
> philosophers and also the idea of a mental substance; and
> establishes the principle that self-consciousness, though not in
> the same degree in every individual, is nevertheless the leading
> principle of mind, that mental evolution consists in enlarging
> our environment, in placing ourselves in proper organic
> relation with the spiritual universe. [5]

Here there are traces of psychology, of Newman Smyth's philosophy, and of Morris's mixing of Aristotle and Hegel.

The experience that seems to have enabled (or forced) Dewey to sort out his thinking at this juncture in his career, to begin to bring the elements in it into a coherent system, was the writing of his first book, the *Psychology* text. He started it, probably, at the end of his first semester at Michigan, around January 1885, and, working on it to the exclusion of practically all other projects, he completed it in a year. Around the time that he finished the manuscript, he published two major articles in which he presented his views on the relationship of psychology to philos-ophy (these were published early in 1886), and within the next year or so he wrote two more pieces defending his views. In January 1888 the University of Minnesota hired him to occupy its chair of philosophy, his duties to begin in September of that year. Psychology as a preoccupation, then, and his first four years at Michigan formed a distinct period in his life, in the course of which he largely established a professional and philosophical identity for himself. [6]

As we saw toward the end of chapter 3, Newman Smyth's

"dynamic intuitionalism" had enabled Dewey to conclude that "modern psychology is intensely ethical in its tendencies." Dewey, having come this far with Smyth, having justified science, had open to him several courses of action that were logically consistent with his and Smyth's conclusions. Although he almost certainly never considered any of them, the alternatives he neglected are worth outlining, if only to establish the nature of the one he chose.

After Smyth and the "New Psychology" Dewey could have— logically, that is—become a laboratory man, pure and simple. That is, good science being good theology, he could have restricted his formal, active existence as an intellectual exclusively to experimentation in a laboratory of physiological psychology— measuring some aspects of neural activity, say. Leaving universal concerns and implications to the philosophers and theologians whose business they were, he would have undertaken simply to achieve an empirical understanding of an aspect of nature through physiological psychology. With Smyth's conclusions in the back of his mind, Dewey could have gone about his work untroubled, knowing that he was providing the raw material for ministers and philosophers to convert into an understanding of God's salvific activity on man.

This was one alternative, but it was not for Dewey. He had chosen philosophy. Six or seven years later, in a letter to William James in 1891, Dewey described himself as having been "led into philosophy and into 'idealism' " by "some sort of instinct, and by the impossibility of my doing anything in particular."[7] It may well have been instinct that led Dewey away from particulars and to the universal, but it was an instinct mediated by more definable elements in his life. He was now very much the disciple of Morris. But he had also experienced Johns Hopkins and G. Stanley Hall and his psychology; empiricism had come to represent to him among other things the possibility of putting a strong new foundation under Morris's Right Hegelianism. Could it be founded on nature itself, could Dewey hitch science to it, so that science's every advance would automatically serve to strengthen that transcendentalism, then would he have *done* something! This was a philosopher's work, not an experimenter's.

Similarly, this objective of Dewey's dictated some of his choices within philosophy. William James's style of philosophizing, for instance, was ruled out for him. James, even at his most partial, tried to discipline himself to ask only whether psychological phenomena could be made to give any evidence tending toward affirmative answers in the traditional concerns of philosophy: free will, our knowledge of reality, the spirituality of the soul, etc. He would, however, take no for an answer; he accepted the inconclusiveness of most facts.

Dewey went to the opposite end of philosophy; he was still bent on defending a structure, and his early ventures into empirical psychology, his writings of the 1880s, were dominated by a relentless impulse toward system. The really striking thing about Dewey's early empiricism is that there was so little of it. In a scathing review of Dewey's first book, the *Psychology* of 1886, G. Stanley Hall commented that,

> Viewed from the standpoint of facts, very few of them are satisfactory, and many we believe to be fundamentally wrong and misleading. . . . But the author is more intent on the mutual interpretation and coherence of his network of definitions than on their relation to facts. [8]

Although it might appear that "dynamic intuitionalism" could have served Dewey in his purposes, this was not the case, for Smyth's philosophy had handicaps that turned Dewey away from it. Some of them were circumstantial. Smyth's purposes had been specifically religious. He had meant his dynamic intuitionalism to be an enrichment of Christian apologetics and theology. Now, although Dewey's personal religious beliefs and his purposes—at least in part—were similar to Smyth's, the theological and devotional character of Smyth's discourse, had Dewey adopted it, would have cast him exactly in the role he most wanted to avoid—that of Christian apologist, a reembodiment of the philosophy professor in the American denominational colleges of the previous half-century. He did not want to come on as Dewey the disciple but as Dewey himself, a scientist among scientists, a philosopher among philosophers. The audience to whom he would be wanting to address himself would be fellow professionals in the university. What he needed was a lingua franca that would present both himself and the culture and beliefs he shared with Smyth to the world of secular learning in a way that was free of the embarrassments and incommunicabilities of prayer and acts of faith and free of any fatal admission that these beliefs needed a special propping and were not really just the best reading of reality, of nature as it presents itself. Thanks doubtless to Morris's presence at Hopkins, Dewey found this language in Hegelianism. In the hands of churchmen like Morris, Hegelianism had already been put to use in just this way: as a means of rendering superfluous a leap of faith in a hidden God. Their Hegelianism demonstrated that God is logically implied in reason and in nature; at its most adventurous it was on the way toward presenting God not as transcendent and utterly other but as the Absolute Idea implying its own complete intelligibility. In short, this Hegelianism saw itself as a theism that could be completely explored and encompassed by reason.

Though Dewey might possibly have acknowledged these situational elements in his rejection of Smyth's philosophy, he most certainly would have pointed out that there were also powerful logical reasons for his decision against Smyth and for Hegel. The basic one, we may guess, was that Dewey found Smyth's epistemology unsatisfactory; for all its "dynamism," it was still an intuitionalism. That is to say, Smyth had presented a plausible and attractive theory about *how* our "real knowledge" of things and the relations among them arises, but his theory still rested on the undemonstrated proposition *that* it is a real knowledge in the first place. Essentially, he had made the same question-begging assertion that the Scottish common-sense realists had made in trying to counter Hume and at the same time avoid Kant's noumenal agnosticism. Thus Smyth on our intuitions: "these constants of reason . . . are not thus mere forms of thought imposed upon things [Kant's doctrine, roughly]; but rather the real relations of things imposing themselves upon any intelligence capable of receiving them."[9] Dewey, much as he sympathized with this conclusion, realized that Smyth had arrived at it by an act of faith, not of reason. Yet Dewey could not let Kant's noumenal agnosticism be the last word either. If he did, he would have let slip away the very justification of science that he had wanted so badly and had found in Smyth. A man studying physiological psychology while holding to a Kantian (or Humean) epistemology could claim only to be clarifying the subjective processes of human cerebration; he could not pretend to be saying anything about the world as it exists, never mind its ends or God's ways in it. He could have no natural theology. His studies would be a form of science for the sake of science.

So what Dewey needed was an epistemological solution that would be philosophically defensible while permitting him the same objective, universal[10] knowledge that Smyth thought his intuitionalism gave him. As he had phrased it in "The New Psychology," he wanted a convincing theory of man's knowledge that would demonstrate "that reality, not necessary *beliefs about* reality, is given in the living experience of the soul's development."[11] Kantianism couldn't do it, because—as Dewey put it— of its acceptance of "the impossibility of solving the problem of philosophy, expressed in the setting up of the unknown thing-in-itself as the ultimate ground and condition of experience."[12] Hegelianism, on the other hand, completed Kant's philosophy where Kant himself had faltered: it claimed that there is no reason to assume that the thing-in-itself is unknowable, and it showed that all reality can be adequately accounted for without appealing to something unknown.

Dewey's reentry into Hegelianism as an empiricist posed a problem, however; for Hegel himself, and after him the British neo-Hegelians from whom Morris derived, had assigned a niche to psychology, a place very similar to its ordinary definition today: "the study of the phenomena of human consciousness and behavior." Dewey outlined the position:

> It is held, or seems to be held, by representatives of the
> post-Kantian movement, that man may be regarded in two
> aspects, in one of which he is an object of experience like
> other objects: with these things he is in relations of action
> and reaction, but possesses the additional characteristic that he
> is a knowing, feeling, willing *phenomenon*. As such, he forms
> the object of a special science, psychology, which, like every
> other special science, deals with its material as pure object,
> abstracting from that creative synthesis *of subject and object*,
> self-consciousness, through which all things are and are known
> [i.e., philosophy's area]. It is therefore, like all the special
> sciences, partial and utterly inadequate to determining the
> nature and meanings of that whole with which philosophy
> has to deal.[13]

So, in this Hegelianism, psychology was just another special science, like chemistry or physics, and dealt with the phenomena of human consciousness, deliberately prescinding from the universal aspect of the human mind by which it is the subject constituting all reality. Had Dewey, while identifying himself as a psychologist, abided by this definition of his role, he would, of course, have been caught in the same dilemma in which Kantianism would have placed him: he would have been studying the phenomena of human mental processes for their own sake and without any formal attempt to see what these phenomena said about objective reality. He would have defined himself as a scientist, but at the cost of forswearing philosophy.

Dewey escaped this predicament by an argument that, though it seems simple enough in outline, was so impressively original as to win for the two essays that contained it placement as lead articles in successive issues of *Mind*, at that time the foremost philosophical and psychological journal in the English-speaking world. His writings acted out his ambitions; these two articles and the textbook, *Psychology*, which he published later that year, lifted Dewey's name out of the Michigan woods and gave him an international scholarly audience and reputation. [14]

Dewey argued that when the Hegelians tried to leave room in their system for an empirical psychology that prescinded from the questions of philosophy, they put themselves in an untenable position. What, Dewey asked, does this nonphilosophical psychology deal with? Everyone would admit that its subject matter, while starting perhaps at the lowest and simplest physiological responses (reflexes and the like), extends at least as far as to include human perception of the most basic sort. But, Dewey pointed out, "those who admit perception would find themselves hard put to it to give a reason for excluding memory, imagination, conception, judgment, reasoning," for all these also are part of human psychic experience, the subject matter of psychology. [15] And why not then also admit self-consciousness (in its Hegelian meaning) into psychology? It is the next stage of mental activity, we *do* experience it, and there is no logical reason to exclude it. Dewey had posed a dilemma to the Hegelians:

> There is no possible break: either we must deny the possibility of treating perception in psychology, and then our "purely objective science of psychology" can be nothing more than a physiology; or, admitting it, we must admit what follows

directly from and upon it—self-consciousness. Self-consciousness is indeed a *fact* (I do not fear the word) of experience,
and must therefore find its treatment in psychology. [16]

Either there is no such thing as an empirical psychology, or it
treats self-consciousness just as it does the rest of conscious
experience. Enormous consequences follow from this latter
alternative. Self-consciousness at its fully developed stage is
man's realization that the world is objectified self. Psychology
then is the study of the realization of the world in consciousness;
but inasmuch as the universe *has* no other existence except as
realized in consciousness, this statement can be reduced to the
more economical phrasing: Psychology is the study of the universe.
The study of the universe, or of all being, is of course philosophy;
therefore psychology *is* philosophy, and John Dewey in his role as
empirical psychologist is the philosopher par excellence!

The fact that Dewey's argument, thus baldly outlined, looks
outrageous, is to the good, for that is how it seems to have struck
the more sophisticated of his contemporaries in philosophy and
philosophical psychology, men like Shadworth H. Hodgson and
William James (the former, confessing his "astonishment" at
Dewey's logical trickery, attempted a refutation of it in a later
issue of *Mind* that year; James simply remarked "poor Dewey"). [17]
However, Dewey's proposal can be put in a way that makes it
look less bizarre and perhaps more plausible to the reader. His
first premise is one that we all accept, namely, that everything we
know comes to us through our mental processes, and psychology
is the systematic scientific study of these processes. Therefore, he
contended, psychology, being the study of the *medium* through
which we know what we know, is also the study of the *content* of
our knowledge. This seems far fetched—unless, that is, the
medium of our knowledge and the content are the same. From
our "common-sense" point of view, most of us would deny this;
we would maintain that the aspects of nature that physics studies,
for example, exist in their own right, "out there," and that our
knowledge of them, our science of physics, is another thing
altogether—certainly, the physical world is not dependent for its
existence on our knowing about it. Still less is the study of the
physicists' psychology, of their thought processes, the study of
physics itself. But this, of course, is exactly the point of Dewey's
Hegelianism. If we put aside for the moment our common-sense

point of view and adopt his premises that everything that exists, exists only in and for consciousness and, second, that every type and branch of knowledge is nothing but a stage in the development of universal mind (physics, for instance, has its place in the Hegelian system as one stage—coming between "Mechanics" and "organics"—in the "Idea-Outside-Itself"), we should find more understandable Dewey's proposal that in scientifically studying consciousness we are studying the universe.

∽

The student of the early writings of Dewey comes after a while to accept that Dewey is going to make his advances toward his later instrumentalism in contexts of retrospection and system-shoring. "Psychology as Philosophic Method" was one of those moments. After he had presented his central argument, which we have reviewed, Dewey pointed out how it would answer the principal criticism directed against classical Hegelianism and in effect redeem that system; at the same time, his argument led him into corollaries that had a conspicuous modernity to them (enough, apparently, to catch the eye of William James, despite his loathing of the Hegelian terminology and his dismissal of Dewey's main point).

The Hegelian system, Dewey wrote, has been dogged by the charge that in using logic for its method of philosophizing it has left itself incapable of dealing with the particular, concrete existences that constitute nature and with the individuals who make up the human race. Hegelianism is able by deduction to trace out the *logical* development of the Idea from the ultimate abstraction of Pure Being, through Essence and the Notion, to its culmination in the presumably concrete "Absolute Idea"; but there is no way for logic to go from these ideas out to the world of particular individual existences: "There is no way of getting from logic to the philosophy of nature *logically*. The only way is to fall back upon the fact: 'we know from experience' that we have nature as well as the *Idee*." By the same token, a philosophy with logic as its method must default when it comes time to deal with individual human beings: "The same is true when we pass to the philosophy of spirit. The general *form* of personality is deducible, but not a living human spirit with its individual thoughts, feelings, and actions."[18] In effect this line of criticism concludes that Hegel does not really deduce the actual world but, rather, covertly uses an aposteriori method, relying, without admitting it, on his actual experience of the world of individual existences to develop his "pure thought." Philosophers such as Friedrich Trendelenburg, Morris's old teacher, rejected Hegelianism for this reason. Dewey, however, saw only a counsel that the idealists ought to come to terms with the fact that their method really is aposteriori, or scientific, and acknowledge that they come to know the real world not through logic but through experience: "In truth, we do not go from logic to nature at all. The movement is a reverse movement."[19] And again he repeated his original point that the scientific, systematic study of experience is psychology: "More definitely, Psychology, and not Logic, is the method of Philosophy."[20]

Once more it was Dewey putting a new foundation under the structure he had inherited. More specifically, in this instance he was saying that his teacher Morris, had he but known, would not have had to enter Hegelianism by way of intellectual reaction and retreat from science: he could have had both worlds, and had them in their mutually sustaining relationship, as Dewey himself now meant to have them.

∽

As though to confirm that this would be Dewey's direction, there was, woven into the same discussion, the most forward-looking argument yet to appear in his writings. What occasioned it was Dewey's defense of his new notion of psychology against the opponent who, while granting that psychology is the science that studies the *manifestation* of the Absolute Idea in individual men (that is, studies how individual men attain to objective, universal knowledge), would argue that true philosophy is something else again: the study of the Absolute Idea itself and not merely the study of its manifestation in individual lives. Dewey responded:

> . . . what *is* this distinction between the absolute self-conscious-ness and its manifestation in a being like man? Is the absolute self-consciousness complete in itself, or does it involve this

realisation and manifestation in a being like man? If it is
complete in itself, how can any philosophy which is limited
to this "absolute principle of self-consciousness" [i.e., any
philosophy that is not Dewey's psychology] face and solve the
difficulties involved in its going beyond itself in self-consciousness [i.e., in individual human lives]? This cannot be what
is meant. . . . [P]*hilosophy under any theory of its nature, can
deal with this absolute self-consciousness only so far as it has
partially and interruptedly realised itself in man. For man, as
object of his philosophy, this Absolute has existence only so
far as it has manifested itself in his conscious experience.*[21]

These last two sentences, taken by themselves, have consequences
identical to those of William James's philosophizing. They ascribe
a singular value to individual experience and seem to say, or
almost to say, that the subject of philosophy really is no longer the
Absolute, but individual experience. William James, when he
was reading Dewey's article, probably wondered why Dewey
didn't then go all the way and dispense altogether with the first
part of the quoted passage—with the *Absolute* self-consciousness.

It was this last step that James was expecting when, several
months after the appearance of "Psychology as Philosophic
Method" in the April 1886 issue of *Mind*, he picked up Dewey's
first book, the *Psychology*, "quite 'enthused' at first glance" and
"hoping for something really fresh." James came away, as he put
it, "sorely disappointed." Dewey had a way to go before he
would be prepared to dismiss the Absolute self-consciousness and
what it implied: objective idealism, a sure demonstration of the
truths of religion, a natural theology, and, for Dewey personally,
a religious faith. His *Psychology* turned out to be a textbook in
that absolute idealism, illustrated and "evidenced" where possible by facts drawn from physiological psychology. James judged
the book a failure ("It's no use trying to mediate between the bare
miraculous self [by which James meant the Absolute self-
consciousness] and the concrete particulars of individual mental
lives; and all that Dewey effects by so doing is to take all the edge
and definiteness away from the particulars when it falls their turn
to be treated"). [22]

If we grant James's criteria, it is hard to argue with his
estimate. Dewey's *Psychology* is a dull book to a modern
sensibility. By and large, it concerned itself with "particulars"
only to the point of typing them or showing that they bear out the

structure of Hegelian epistemology. The book was at an infinite remove from the virtuosity of James's *Principles of Psychology*, which was being written at the same time. Yet, when all this has been said, it is hard not to feel that such criticism is beside the point. Dewey indicated in his preface what criteria he wanted his *Psychology* judged by: he had written the book "expressly for use in class-room instruction," the classrooms of "our colleges," where "it is the custom ... to make psychology the path by which to enter the fields of philosophy."[23] And the book *was* effective in this role. "When I got to college," reminisced an 1890 alumnus of the University of Michigan,

> I went on with the classical course, but after my freshman year I began to have opportunity for election and seized the earliest opportunity to get into logic and psychology. The logic which was based on Jevons' well-known little book interested me, though it did not greatly excite me. But the psychology (Dewey's recently published text) instantly opened up a new world, which it seemed to me I had been waiting for, and for the first time I felt a deep and pervasive sense of the intellectual importance of the material I was facing. ... I had never before encountered anything which seemed to afford me the sense of grasp, insight, and mastery in a subject intrinsically of crucial significance. With that experience began my real intellectual life. [24]

The old textbooks of "philosophical psychology"—Noah Porter's and John Bascom's books, with their notions of human faculties— were being discredited by the "New Psychology" of the German universities and laboratories. Dewey knew this, and his textbook was meant to fill the gap; for the colleges still existed, and the college culture itself was still very much alive to Dewey, even if it did need to be led out of darkness. With the wisdom of hindsight, we can now say that Dewey was moving out of the one world into the other; but in 1885, when he wrote his textbook, Dewey saw himself rather as bringing the two worlds together. It was this mission of Dewey's that was behind a good deal of the confusion in his *Psychology* as to where physiology ended and psychology began and where the latter ended and philosophy began.[25] Just as Dewey was the mediator between university and college, trying to personify both worlds, so was his precious psychology the mediator between physiology and philosophy or, if you like, between science and theology. Needless to say, nobody would listen. Hall sneered at Dewey's metaphysics; and when, in another review of the book, Dewey's old college teacher, H. A. P. Torrey, caught Dewey saying, "Psychologically speaking, the world is objectified self; the self is subjectified world," he clucked his demurral: "*Metaphysically* speaking, rather we would say."[26]

As for the part of Dewey that was still college-bound and expressing itself in system-building or defending, it is hard not to be as impatient with it as Hall and James were and to see it as something to be "got over" in the interests of his later full-fledged experimentalism. Actually, though, Dewey never got over it. Some of it he transformed: the Hegelian doctrine that has the individual reproducing the universal consciousness, he later noted, helped rid him of the assumption that man has a "ready-made mind set over against a physical world as an object" and helped convince him "that the only possible psychology, as distinct from a biological account of behavior, is a social psychology."[27] Some of this drive toward system, the deepest substrate of it, never really left him. As a philosopher he remained a systematizer; what new principles and methods he discovered he submitted to the test of universal applicability. He addressed his instrumentalism to society, politics, religion and morality, the arts, education—all of them. This was a legacy of his Hegelianism. More accurately, it was the persistence of what had brought him and Morris to Hegel: a notion of philosophy as the expression and defense of an ethos and not merely as a way of dealing with the theoretical problems arising in a particular, limited institutional setting, such as the laboratories of the sciences or the issue-oriented dialogues of modern academic philosophy and its journals. This is not to say that technical or academic philosophers do not occasionally take on such a universal task but rather that, objectively, it is not expected of them and, subjectively, it is not essential to their conception of themselves as philosophers. In Dewey's case it was, and not to have done it would have been, however subtly or pardonably, to default.

Dewey's moralism, his unconscious assumption that philosophy should not only describe but prescribe, was similarly grounded. It is impossible to imagine Dewey ever sharing James's considerable playfulness of intellect, his interest in the singular and the odd, or the dominant individualism of James's outlook. Implicit in James's complaint that Dewey's *Psychology*, in its concentration on the Absolute, took "all the edge and definiteness away from the particulars" was Dewey's inability to write a book like *The Varieties of Religious Experience*, a study of lonely and extraordinary experiences, and James's corresponding profound lack of interest in "a common faith." James was a cosmopolitan and a pluralist in both temperament and upbringing. He never expected anything other than a really radical diversity in the world. Dewey, by contrast, was a provincial, and what he was after was the normal in that word's full meaning.

5 Ethics

Dewey had been in his new post at the University of Minnesota not a year when George Sylvester Morris unexpectedly died and the trustees of the University of Michigan invited Dewey back to fill Morris's position. That fall, 1889, Dewey returned to Ann Arbor. The first thing Dewey wrote for publication when he returned was a four-page outline of the ethics curriculum to be offered in his department; he submitted the outline to the *Ethical Record*, an Ethical Culture Society magazine then about a year and a half old. [1] The outline set several of the themes for the next five years. To begin with, in choosing to publish in the *Ethical Record*, Dewey gave notice of what was to be a definitive change of audience on his part. Except for a handful of book reviews and one commencement address, which he published in the *Andover Review*, Dewey now stopped appearing in theological journals altogether. [2] Instead, he published most of his major statements of this period (excepting, of course, the books) in journals associated with the Ethical Culture movement: the *Ethical Record*, the *International Journal of Ethics*, *Open Court*, and the *Monist*. [3] This was more than a simple rejection of religious organs; it signaled a change of subject also, for Dewey's principal writings of those years were in fact almost all on the problems of ethical philosophy. He was concentrating his teaching in that area, and the two books he wrote were the 1891 *Outlines of a Critical Theory of Ethics* and the 1894 *The Study of Ethics: a Syllabus*. The third theme the outline touched on was expressed only indirectly, but very clearly, in its last paragraph, when Dewey apologized for the paucity of offerings in ethics at Michigan that year:

> . . . with but two instructors it is impossible to do much special work in ethics without the neglect of other departments in philosophy. Another year a course will probably be offered in

the Ethics of Plato, Kant, or Hegel. [Within a year or two
they all were.] The limited amount of work in ethics has been
less noticeable in the past because of the profound ethical
spirit in which the lamented Professor Morris carried on all
his work in philosophy, and which he imparted so successfully
to all his instruction. [4]

Dewey was serving notice that the "profound ethical spirit" of
Morris would now be replaced by a professional, academic
treatment of ethics—that the ethics courses at the university
would henceforth be distinguished once and for all from the
ethics of the pulpit and would be treated, as befitted any
university subject, scientifically. In effect, under his chairman-
ship, ethics would be subjected to the same process that in the
previous five years he had applied to the problems of epistemology and metaphysics. In these areas his tool had been the
"science" of psychology; now it would be the science of ethics. [5]

Dewey had in fact published a statement on ethics during his
first years at Michigan, an article he titled "Ethics and Physical
Science."[6] In it he took up the cudgels against those mechanistic
philosophers (again, Lewes, Spencer, and company) who were
attempting to construct an ethical theory on the grounds of
physical science alone. Dewey had in mind the type of system
that tried to find the basis for ethical behavior in the fact that
men, like the rest of nature, are subject to evolution; specifically,
he wanted to combat the claim that men come to recognize that
the "good" is the onward march of evolution and that their
"moral" behavior consists in cooperating to further that progress.
"In spite of the vigor and ardor with which these ideas are
urged," Dewey wrote, "some of us at least, remain unmoved. We
believe that the cause of theology and morals is one, and that
whatever banishes God from the heart of things, with the same
edict excludes the ideal, the ethical, from the life of man." Dewey
acknowledged that his position (still very much Green's and
Morris's) demanded that he do two things: first, show that ethics
"is not compatible with a physical interpretation of reality" and,
second, show that it is "compatible only with a spiritual interpretation, which in its broad and essential features is identical with
the theological teaching of Christianity." Dewey excused himself
from this latter metaphysical chore on this occasion and never
dealt with it subsequently. [7]

In the course of fulfilling his first task, however (that is, in the course of showing that ethics has no place in a physical interpretation of reality), Dewey did indicate more clearly what this positive half of his defense against the claims of the physical evolutionists would have to effect. The "fundamental fallacy," he said, in the ethical theories of the materialists is that they assume what they have to prove: they busy themselves with trying to show how there evolved a recognition in men that the wisest selfishness is altruism—that is, they attempt to find the mechanism by which men came to recognize that the most effective form of self-interest is the pursuit of the common good. What they fail to see is "that this assumes the whole point at issue, the very nerve of the discussion, viz., the *existence* of an identity of interests and the more or less conscious recognition of it."[8] Not only can this not be taken for granted by the physical evolutionists, Dewey insisted, but their own way of looking at the world demands the opposite conclusion. Their hypothesis is one of struggle for existence: "Those best fitted to the environment survive; those less fitted go to the wall. Rivalry, struggle, is thus the very heart of the physical process."[9] Any attempt, then, to build an ethical system on physical science is doomed. It is only by way of a metaphysic that establishes that the universe is ruled by a benevolent intelligence that a consistent ethical system can be constructed. Only then is a man justified in saying that slaughter and waste are not real but apparent or are means to a larger good, and only then can he say that the good of all humanity is his own highest good.

This was in 1887. In 1891 Dewey brought out with the Register Publishing Company of Ann Arbor a little book called *Outlines of a Critical Theory of Ethics*.[10] (Dewey noted in the preface that the book had "taken shape in connection with class-room work," and it matches so closely the description of the ethics courses he submitted to the *Ethical Record* two years before that it is plain that the book was a distillation of what he had worked out in his teaching.) Toward the middle of the *Outlines*, Dewey came to deal with the same problem he had discussed in "Ethics and Physical Science," but the treatment was, to say the least, strikingly different from the earlier one.

In the first half of the book Dewey had examined and rejected various notions of "the good" and had finally arrived at what by his lights was the only adequate one, namely, that the "end of action, or the good, is the realized will, the developed or satisfied self."[11] He then went on to enumerate some of the modes of self-realization and to suggest that these various self-fulfilling activities also in fact work toward the *common* good, his argument here being that man is intrinsically social, that his relationship to society at large is organic—like that of the eye to the body—and that what benefits the member benefits the entire organism. At this point, however, Dewey granted that he could not prove this for any given case and that

> in most, if not all cases, the agent acts from a faith that, in
> realizing his own capacity, he will satisfy the needs of society.
> If he were asked to *prove* that his devotion to his function
> were right because certain to promote social good, he might
> well reply: "That is none of my affair. I have only to work
> myself out as strength and opportunity are given me, and let
> the results take care of themselves. I did not make the world,
> and if it turns out that devotion to the capacity which was
> given me, and loyalty to the surroundings in which I find
> myself do not result in good, I do not hold myself responsible.
> But, after all, I cannot believe that it will so turn out. What
> is really good for me *must* turn out good for all, or else
> there is no good in the world at all." The basis, in a word,
> of moral conduct, with respect to the exercise of function, is
> a faith that moral self-satisfaction . . . means social satisfac-
> tion—or the faith that self and others make a true community.[12]

This, of course, is the same statement of an ethical order that Dewey in 1887 had accused the mechanist ethical philosophers of assuming (when, he said, they should have been proving it). On that earlier occasion he had implied that objective idealism could definitely establish an ethical order. Now he had found a third way of handling the issue by making the ethical order a *postulate* in the Kantian sense: a necessary presupposition of action or of the willingness to act.[13] He had quietly moved away from neo-Hegelianism and was now going about the task of estab-lishing an ethics from a position of theological or metaphysical agnosticism. He acknowledged this backhandedly when he added:

> In calling it a postulate we do not mean to call it unprovable,
> much less unverifiable, for moral experience is itself, so far as
> it goes, its verification. But we do mean that the further

consideration of this postulate, its demonstration or (if the case so be) its refutation, do not belong to the realm of ethics as such. Each branch of human experience rests upon some presupposition which, *for that branch*, is ultimate. The further inquiry into such presuppositions belongs not to mathematics, or physics, or ethics, but to metaphysics. [14]

And Dewey was through with metaphysics. (As he was to write to his young friend James Rowland Angell two years later, "metaphysics has had its day, and if the truths which Hegel saw cannot be stated as direct, practical truths, they are not true.")[15] However, in refounding the ethical order as a postulate, he was not merely grasping at a straw or availing himself of a handy stratagem. He had a specific model in mind, and it is a revealing one. An analogous postulate, he noted, is made in the realm of the sciences:

All science rests upon the conviction [or postulate] of the thorough-going and permanent unity of the world of objects known—a unity sometimes termed the "uniformity of nature" or the "reign of law"; without this conviction that objects are not mere isolated and transitory appearances, but are connected together in a system by laws or relations, science would be an impossibility. [16]

Not only does this postulate make science possible, it makes it possible without a metaphysics. This is how men do science: they postulate an order in the phenomenal world and then attempt by experiment to ascertain what it is. This instinctive, natural procedure is correct and shrewd. It is the same in ethics, Dewey was suggesting: this is how men behave, and philosophers should realize it.

∞

The implications of this new tack of Dewey's had already been spelled out by the time the *Outlines* came out in 1891, for in January of that year he had published an essay, "Moral Theory and Practice," in the second number of the new *International Journal of Ethics*, which one way or another told most of the story of Dewey's new moral philosophy. Dewey had been provoked into writing his statement by four articles that had

appeared in the first issue of the *Journal*. Two in particular
irritated him, Felix Adler's "The Freedom of Ethical Fellowship"
and William M. Salter's "A Service of Ethics to Philosophy."[17] As
Dewey said, "rather than seek some more impersonal, and
therefore more remote, form of statement," he chose "to let the
tensions discharge as they first arose."[18]

Salter, at one point in his essay, had said:

> he who admits ethical ideas into the circle of his belief can
> never be content with strictly "scientific" philosophy. So far as
> scientific means clearness and systematic arrangement of con-
> ceptions, he will, of course, crave scientific philosophy and no
> other; but so far as "scientific" denotes reliance on observation
> and experiment, so far as "scientific philosophy" is put forth as
> a new method of philosophizing, it must inevitably be re-
> garded as incomplete. Beyond the realm of what is and
> happens, ethics opens up another realm of what ought to be.
> Alongside of every man, of every action, of every institution,
> of every social order, is the notion of what they should be. [19]

Dewey—correctly—found lurking in such statements the "idea
that moral conduct is something other than, or over and above,
conduct itself."[20] He seemed to be aware that this fugitive notion
about moral conduct is the one most commonly held, consciously
and unconsciously, by philosophers and laymen alike, and he
decided that the best way to smoke it out would be to begin the
inquiry with moral *theory*. "What, then, is moral theory?"
he asked.

> It is all one with moral *insight*, and moral insight is the
> recognition of the relationships in hand. This is a very tame
> and prosaic conception. It makes moral insight, and therefore
> moral theory, consist simply in the every-day workings of the
> same ordinary intelligence that measures dry-goods, drives
> nails, sells wheat, and invents the telephone. There is no more
> halo about the insight that determines what I should do in
> this catastrophe of life when the foundations are upheaving
> and my bent for eternity lies waiting to be fixed, than in
> that which determines whether commercial conditions favor
> heavy or light purchases. There is nothing more divine or
> transcendental in resolving how to save my degraded neighbor
> than in the resolving of a problem in algebra, or in the mastery
> of Mill's theory of induction. [21]

Dewey's conception of moral theory as the same "every-day workings of the same ordinary intelligence that measures dry-goods" may have seemed to him "a very tame and prosaic conception," but he must have known that to those of his readers familiar with philosophy it would be seen as a very extraordinary one indeed. Those who missed this quality in it the first time around surely saw it when, later in the article, Dewey showed what his theory would mean in a concrete situation:

> Let us take, then, a specific case: Here is a street-car con-ductor, and the question is whether he should (ought to) join in a strike which his Union has declared. I do not intend to make and resolve some hypothetical case, but simply, in order to get out of that undoubtedly adorable, yet somewhat vague, realm to which we so naturally incline when we discuss obligation, call up the kind of fact which constitutes obliga-tion. The man thinks of his special work, with its hardships, indeed, and yet a work, an activity, and thus a form of free-dom or satisfaction; he thinks of his wage, of what it buys; of his needs, his clothing, his food, his beer and pipe. He thinks of his family, and of his relations to them; his need of pro-tecting and helping them on; his children, that he would educate, and give an evener start in the world than he had himself; he thinks of the families of his fellows: of the need that they should live decently and advance somewhat; he thinks of his bonds to his Union; he calls up the way in which the families of the corporation which employs him live; he tries to realize the actual state of business, and imagines a possible failure and its consequences, and so on. Now where in this case do we get beyond concrete facts, and what is the "ought" but the outcome of these facts, varying as the facts vary, and expressing simply and only the situation which the facts form, so far as our man has the intelligence to get at it? And how does this case differ from any case of moral action?

"What," Dewey demanded, "has become of moral rules and laws in this case?"

> A man's duty is never to obey certain rules; his duty is always to respond to the nature of the actual demands which he finds made upon him,—demands which do not proceed from ab-stract rules, nor from ideals, however awe-inspiring and exalted, but from the concrete relations to men and things in which he finds himself. [22]

Plainly, there were difficulties in Dewey's proposals regarding moral theory and practice.[23] Some of them show up quite clearly in Dewey's own example. The streetcar conductor, whether he knows it or not, has other decisions to make than simply whether to strike or not, and some of these will involve him in choosing among theories in a way that Dewey's philosophy seems not to have taken into account. In presenting the case as he did, Dewey plainly meant for the givens of the situation to dictate one response and one response only—to strike. If this conclusion were indeed ineluctable, then Dewey's insistence that "the every-day workings" of the "ordinary intelligence" are an adequate guide would be confirmed. But what if his workingman had listened to an anarchist orator the day before, and what if, as a result, he was bothered with such questions as how and when to strike, whether to strike for a pay increase or for the overthrow of an evil social system, whether to strike violently or not, whether to kill the owners or not? Worse, what if someone else had suggested to him that the common good is to be found not in a leveling equality but in "social order"? Or if some economist had told him the empirical evidence suggested that in the long run the greatest common good would be fostered by the temporary continuance of the present exploitation of him and his fellow workers?

Now it is conceivable that Dewey's "practical consciousness" could be extended to the point where it could deal with some of these problems, but that would be going counter to the whole spirit and point of Dewey's philosophy here. Dewey made that perfectly clear a page or two later, when he was warning against Salter's notion (and nearly everyone's notion, for that matter) that ethics has somehow to do with a "realm of what ought to be" as distinguished from "the realm of what is and happens."[24] As an example of one of Salter's ethical "ideals," Dewey suggested justice:

> Let, for example, our conductor be fixed upon justice. Now, just so far as he is able to resolve "justice" into specific relations between men and men, so far he will have a definite end in view, and such emotions as are aroused within him will simply quicken him in his effort to realize these relations. But just so far as he cannot translate "justice" into such actual relations, so far it becomes a sentiment,—it is justice in general, at large. And this sentiment is almost sure to turn into a bitterness of

feeling which leads astray,—to a blind feeling that things
should be overturned because they are not what they should
be.[25]

This is typical of Dewey's thinking. Where thought and action
cannot be "definite" or "concrete" or "direct," the result will be a
morbid state in the subject; and when Dewey is talking about
thought and action having to do immediately with social issues,
this psychopathology will find one of two expressions: either
pious wringing of hands or revolution.[26] To say then, in defense
of Dewey's claims for the powers of the "ordinary intelligence
that measures dry-goods," that it can be sufficiently elaborated to
deal with such questions as we have put in the head of our
streetcar conductor, is to save the philosophy at the cost of losing
its point. Dewey wanted a quick and simple guide.

It was the same with the other standard criticism of Dewey's
ethical thought: that it failed to come to terms with the problem
of ethical ideals because it unconsciously relied on these ideals
while denying their presence or even their existence. As I pointed
out in the first part of this chapter, Dewey's way of dealing with
this issue was more direct and sophisticated than it is often
credited with being: in *Outlines of a Critical Theory of Ethics* he
acknowledged that he was postulating the identity of the individual good with the common good, and he had a specific and
honorable model in the scientific postulate (whether it was in the
end a valid model is another question). Yet to overstress this
instance, where he dealt so directly with the problem of ideals,
would again be to save the philosophy at the cost of losing the
point and the man. For instance, when Dewey set pen to paper to
write his rejoinder to Salter and the others for the *International
Journal of Ethics*, his book, with its explanation of his "ethical
postulate," was still in press, and it is very likely that he knew it
would not be published by the time the article appeared.
Furthermore, he can hardly have expected many of his readers in
the *Journal* to have access to the little book, which was being
brought out principally for use in his classrooms by the Inland
Press (Register Publishing Company) of Ann Arbor, Michigan.
Despite this, Dewey made no explicit mention in his article of his
postulate. It is assumed throughout, and it slips unseen from one
section to another, always there when Dewey needs it but never
visible. In the case of the streetcar conductor, for instance, there

is nothing in what Dewey says or implies that would answer the objection that the resolution of the case involves the judgment that the workingman's right to comfort for his family takes precedence over the capitalist's right to his property. This judgment, surely partaking of the realm of the ideal and the theoretical (in the grand sense), is simply taken for granted by Dewey. The closest he comes to dealing with such matters explicitly is in his remark that maxims like the Golden Rule and ideals like truthfulness, and so forth, have—somehow or other (he never says)—arisen out of the aggregate of human experience through the ages. [27] Needless to say, this only begs the question How did they arise? Some such metaphor as "distillation" just won't do for an answer; the process has to be explained. Dewey, however, was most eager not to get into such discussions, and his essay was peppered with such dismissals-in-disguise as his comment, ". . . it is hardly necessary, I suppose, to profess the deepest respect for the Golden Rule." [28] It was hardly adequate, either.

∞

The intellectual sources of Dewey's ethical doctrine are not hard to find. The Hegelianism had a lot to do with it, especially in regard to the content of Dewey's "ethical postulate." The Hegelian idea of reality or the universe or history being the realization of the eternal Idea leads very easily into a conviction that what works for the good of any given individual must tend to the good of the whole. If the world is the expression of a rational, intelligible plan, there is no room in it for true irreconcilables, for stark conflicts. It must all make sense if seen whole; it can't at once be rational and harbor self-contradictions. [29] Dewey's scientific habits of thought, his immersion in physiological psychology and biology, played a large part also. Time and again Dewey relied on psychological models to buttress his ethical arguments. His description of the streetcar conductor finding himself unable to "resolve" his impulse and felt need into a specific action and therefore lapsing into bitter, pathological behavior derives much of its rhetorical power from its reference to the psychological model of a repressed impulse turning in on itself and becoming morbid. Likewise, Dewey was constantly slipping from one use of the word "normal" to the other. In one sentence it is a textbook scientific description of a basic model of human behavior (for instance, impulse translating straight into action, with no hesitation and no complications); in the next sentence it becomes a prescription for how men *ought* to be able to behave.

Dewey's sources and his reasoning are easily enough analyzed. Yet one comes to suspect that this is not really what the situation calls for. Dewey himself gave every indication that it is not. We can see, in his simple neglect to mention the postulate logically underlying his whole argument in "Moral Theory and Practice" or in the impatient crackling of his prose when he was engaged in laying out the argument behind his position, that Dewey is really bent on setting free a notion of his about ethical conduct and that laying the speculative foundations for his idea—having it out with the philosophers, so to speak—was a terribly irritating, inhibiting business for him.*

"Moral Theory and Practice," for instance, takes wing only at the end, when Dewey has done his arguing and feels free at last to depict exactly what it is that he has in mind, his vision:

> Imagine a scene of ceaseless movement; needs, relations, institutions ever moving on. In the midst of this scene appears an intelligence who identifies himself with the wonderful spectacle of action. He finds that its law is his law, because he is only as a member sharing in its needs, constituted by its relations and formed in its institutions. This intelligence would know this scene that he may know himself. He puts forth his grasp, his *Begriff*, and arrests the movement. Taking the movement at a certain point and holding it there, intelligence cuts a cross-section through it to see what it is like. It has now mastered the situation, the case "is" thus and so. Then intelligence removes its brake, its abstracting hold, and the scene moves on. That to which intelligence sees it moving is the "ought to be." The "ought to be" is the larger and fuller activity into which it is the destiny and glory of the present fact to pass. [30]

*Witness the tone of the little soliloquy we quoted earlier from the *Outlines*, when Dewey has the man reply, who is challenged as to whether what he is doing really does make for the common good: "That is none of my affair. I have only to work myself out as strength and opportunity are given me, and let the results take care of themselves. I did not make the world" (Dewey, *Outlines*, p. 127).

The fact that Dewey was a notably restrained philosopher and not given to self-portraiture makes this passage all the more remarkable. Yet it is typical of his ethical writings in his last five years at Michigan: "Moral Theory and Practice" and the other articles—"Green's Theory of the Moral Motive" and "Self-Realization as the Moral Ideal"—together with the book he published in 1894, *The Study of Ethics: a Syllabus*. [31] There is a new man moving through all of them, and if Dewey's philosophy had never been so muddled, neither had his voice ever been so clear. He obviously had achieved a series of personal and intellectual resolutions and perhaps for the first time had an integrated idea of himself and his institutional identity. The integration was so thorough that it is difficult to know where to take hold of it in order to outline it; but in light of the fact that it was a search for "method" that started Dewey philosophizing for himself at Johns Hopkins and in the early years at Michigan, it might be fitting to start there.

Dewey, it will be recalled, had been impressed by the scientific method as early, perhaps, as his second semester at Hopkins. One could cite numerous ways in which he gave away the fact that, rather soon, "method" for him came to be synonymous with scientific method; to mention just one, there was his attempt in his articles in *Mind* to establish science as the method for psychology, and psychology as the method for doing philosophy. [32] His attraction to science had several definable bases. It promised definitive, verifiable, "hard" answers to questions that bore on the issues of philosophy; it promised to end, once and for all, at least *some* arguments in philosophy and thus enable philosophers, like practitioners in other university departments, to claim "progress" in their discipline; and by these means it would secure philosophy's (and the philosopher's) place within the dynamics and structure of the university as that institution was being defined in late-nineteenth-century America. By the time of his first book on ethics, the *Outlines*, Dewey was declaring metaphysics out of bounds for himself and was attempting to put ground under his feet by way of a postulate, much as the scientist did.

Dewey in effect was revisiting the crossroads he had come to several years earlier in the matter of psychology and metaphysics. He could have confessed the inability of empiricism to deal with the questions posed in metaphysics. Had he done this, he could either have identified himself as a scientist and have implicitly or explicitly acknowledged, as he seemed to do in the passage in the *Outlines of Ethics* that we discussed on pages 72–73, that in this identity he would be unable to deal with a number of questions of great importance (that is to say, he could have accepted the role to which Morris had always wanted to relegate scientists), or he could have despaired of his quest for a single method and have maintained his identity as a professional philosopher *and* a scientist by employing the tools of both traditional system-building metaphysics and modern empirical science—two distinct methods.

Dewey chose another direction. He decided to claim omnicompetence for his method. Some of the effects of this we have already mentioned. Having decided that this empiricism could deal with all real issues, and being faced with the fact that it could not deal with the transcendent ("abstract laws" or, as he put it, the idea that " 'justice' and 'love' are ... something in themselves which somehow rule over and sanctify the rest of reality—morally lawless and unsanctified in itself"), he simply decided that the "transcendent" is not real and that the genesis of the conviction that it is can be accounted for historically and behaviorally and thus explained away.[33] The result is that ideals appear in his ethical writings of this period only in a sublimated form; they are there, but their presence is not acknowledged. Instead, all moral problems, Dewey claims, yield to simple workaday "analysis." As for the "ought," the transcendent ethical ideal:

> [that] creaking, lumbering *Deus ex machina* which in the nick of time projects its proper entity upon the stage of human knowledge has ... so often been replaced by the smooth, swift workings of a single intelligence, that we may gather courage for the hope that the "ought" too is from intelligence rather than a somewhat let down from supernal flies or sprung from an unearthly trap.[34]

"The smooth, swift workings of a single intelligence": Dewey by his ethical doctrine had created a new institutional and professional self-concept. G. Stanley Hall had customarily finished his week of laboratory work by going on Sundays to preach in church or Sunday school; he had in effect admitted by this act that there might be two realms and two competences, that science can describe the phenomenal realm but that only theology or metaphysics is in touch with the noumenal and in a position to prescribe conduct. This was exactly the cleavage that Dewey meant to avoid by bringing all these areas into the province of science and the university; he was attempting to keep alive the archetypal notion of the savant in the culture in which he had been raised, the figure of the Professor of Mental and Moral Philosophy. He was trying to have Gilman's university and the dynamic of science without having to accept the judgment that they are, of themselves, amoral. It was an extension of his drive, five years earlier, to identify himself as a scientist and at the same time to keep his identity as a systematic philosopher. Then he had been in pursuit of a scientific metaphysics; [35] now it was a scientific ethics that he was after.

Beneath this integration of his cultural identity one senses that Dewey had effected another type of resolution, a more intimately personal one. In a contribution he made to the *Monthly Bulletin* of the Student Christian Association in 1886, called "The Place of Religious Emotion," Dewey had protested that "Religious feeling is unhealthy when it is watched and analyzed to see if it exists, if it is right, if it is growing. It is as fatal to be forever examining our own religious moods and experiences, as it is to pull up a seed from the ground to see if it is growing." [36] Writers have been quick to put this together with Dewey's recollections of the sense of guilt, the potentially morbid introspection encouraged in him by his mother and her evangelicalism ("which in practice was something worse than Puritanism," he is supposed to have said). [37] Significantly, the theme recurs in "Moral Theory and Practice":

> People are somewhat tired of hearing, "you ought to do thus and so." This condition of fatigue may be due to the depravity of human nature; but I think it is rather due to its goodness; human nature refuses to be moved except in the one truly human way,—through intelligence. Get the fresher, more open outlook, the refined and clarified intelligence, and the emotions will take care of themselves. They *are* there, and all they need is freeing. [38]

In "The Place of Religious Emotion" Dewey's point had been that if "we cultivate humility in the presence of the perfect and matchless character of Christ, we shall find that regret and remorse for our own shortcomings will come quickly enough without our going to pump them up artificially." Here, however, thanks to Dewey's new ethics, the lesson has changed dramatically; now, "Moral conduct is precisely that which realizes an idea, a conception."[39] Moral conduct, that is to say, is human conduct, and vice-versa. Or, again, "Morality is activity, exercise of function."[40] Dewey had, so to speak, exorcised the evangelical conscience; he had dismissed that inner voice (the expression of what Morris in his unhappier moments in the 1870s had called "the double life of the soul")[41] that demanded, "Am I doing right?" or, in his mother's memorable question, "Are you right with Jesus?" He had done it not by cultivating in himself an indifference to morality (that would have been betrayal, and it might backfire and bring remorse) but by coming to see that all human behavior is good behavior.

It was this second achievement of Dewey's, his molding of a new free conscience, that finally brought William James to him. James wrote Dewey an appreciative response to the *Outlines of Ethics* (Dewey presumably had sent him a copy as soon as the book was published), and Dewey replied:

MY DEAR PROFESSOR JAMES,—
Your hearty note regarding the *Ethics* was very welcome to me. The book has received a little of what is called "favorable comment" as well as more or less of the reverse, but so far as reported you are the first man to see the point,—and that I suppose is the dearest thing to a writer. The present preceptual structure is so great, and such a weighty thing, both in theory and in practice, that I don't anticipate any success for the book, but when one man like yourself expresses what you wrote me, the book has already succeeded.
But unless a man is already living in the gospel and not under the law, as you express it, words thrown at him are idle wind. He does n't [sic] understand what you mean, and he would n't [sic] believe you meant it, if he did understand. The hope seems to be with the rising generation. ... Many of my students, I find, are fairly hungering. They almost jump at any opportunity to get out from under the load and to believe in their own lives.[42]

It was shy autobiography, and Dewey begged James's pardon for "the somewhat confessional character" of the letter; but, as he said, "the man who has seen the point arouses the confessional attitude." Dewey's students also saw the point. Several years later one of them who had been in Dewey's courses at this time closed a letter to a former classmate by reminding him, "Dewey used to say that Jesus and Paul taught that man *is* saved. Man *is* what he *shall* be, and what he *ought* to be. He is full of divine possibilities—nay, of divine *certainties*." [43]

James, with his particular concerns and preoccupations, undoubtedly sensed also the element of mind cure in Dewey's reconstruction of ethics. It was as though Dewey, who was gifted with, or perhaps had attained, prodigious powers of concentration, wished to impart such healthy-mindedness to others. In a review he wrote several years after this, he warned that an overemphasis of the personal element in conduct "can end only in useless complications, weariness of the flesh and spirit and contradictions between our aspirations and our accomplishments." He did not make precisely clear what he meant by this excessive "devotion to persons," contenting himself with contrasting it to the better way—"devotion to work, to action and to persons, whether one's self or others, indirectly through their implications in activity." [44] And so Dewey built into his pragmatism a repugnance for antinomies, imponderables, hesitations, distractions, worries; it was, he said, "a theory which makes activity the final word." [45]

∽

Even in his first blush of enthusiasm for the new ethics, Dewey could not entirely forget that there were problems with it. His friend Thomas Davidson asked whether Dewey hadn't put forward an ethics without morality, without a way of distinguishing right from wrong. "There is no morality in my ethics," Dewey answered, "i.e., there is no *apart* morality. Good conduct (once conduct is defined as activity which is an end *to* itself) seems to me a pleonasm." [46] It was a bold statement, but nevertheless Dewey *had* begun to qualify it: "once conduct is defined as activity which is an end to itself. . . ." It would make an interesting study to trace the different formulas Dewey would turn to as the years went by in his attempts to account for the existence of good conduct and bad conduct without drawing his criterion from somewhere outside conduct itself. He was no fool; he knew there are bad things done in this world. How to account for it without fracturing his theory? Is it that "bad" conduct is "not an end to itself," is "incomplete" or "not adequate to the situation," or what?

This was a problem in his ethics, but it was for that very reason an asset. Not having a transcendental ethic to "let down from supernal flies" drove Dewey into extended examination of human conduct and society. The definition of virtue that seems eventually to have most satisfied him was conduct that served society's end: "the genuinely moral person is one, then, in whom the habit of regarding all capacities and habits of self from the social standpoint is formed and active."[47] Correspondingly, he came to focus more and more on man's sociality, the mechanisms by which individual man internalizes the interests and norms of his community. Out of this nucleus issued some of pragmatism's best contributions to our culture: its educational theories and experiments, particularly those concerning young children; the suggestion of Dewey's great colleague George Herbert Mead as to the psychological and social-psychological mechanisms that, he argued, make the human self primarily and intrinsically social; and Dewey's own contributions to the theory of liberal society. In 1927 he wrote:

> . . . to learn to be human is to develop through the give-and-take of communication an effective sense of being an individually distinctive member of a community; one who understands and appreciates its beliefs, desires and methods, and who contributes to a further conversion of organic powers into human resources and values. But this translation is never finished. The old Adam, the unregenerate element in human nature, persists. It shows itself wherever the method obtains of attaining results by use of force instead of by the method of communication and enlightenment. It manifests itself more subtly, pervasively and effectually when knowledge and the instrumentalities of skill which are the product of communal life are employed in the service of wants and impulses which have not themselves been modified by reference to a shared interest. To the doctrine of "natural" economy which held that

commercial exchange would bring about such an interdependence that harmony would automatically result, Rousseau gave an adequate answer in advance. He pointed out that interdependence provides just the situation which makes it possible and worth while for the stronger and abler to exploit others for their own ends, to keep others in a state of subjection where they can be utilized as animated tools. . . .

[T]he only possible solution [is] the perfecting of the means and ways of communication of meanings so that genuinely shared interest in the consequences of interdependent activities may inform desire and effort and thereby direct action. This is the meaning of the statement that the problem is a moral one dependent upon intelligence and education. [48]

Dewey's summary here shows both the strength and the weakness of his approach. It presented a good philosophy for programs of intelligent amelioration, but it said nothing about basic, ineluctable conflict of interests in a society. His philosophy, finally, would not face the possibility that society might *not* be organic, that the ethical postulate might not be true, that the most perspicacious, well-intentioned seeking of one's own good might actually work to the detriment of society at large.

This is why Randolph Bourne was eventually able to say that instrumentalism "had no place for the inexorable,"[49] and it was what made Dewey the philosopher par excellence of American liberalism: he shared with it the root conviction that we can have *both* self-defined self-fulfillment for each individual and social justice for all.

Publics, Politics

On 1 November 1884, back during Dewey's first semester as a faculty member at the University of Michigan, the student newspaper carried the following:

> A very interesting discussion concerning the exact nature of perception was held on Friday in the 9:30 section of Dr. Dewey's class in psychology. At the close of the recitation the prevailing opinion seemed to be that perception is a complex, presentative and representative, premeditatively unconstitutional, excruciatingly metaphysical and utterly incomprehensible act or process of discrimination, localization, and superposition to react upon the same, thus reducing the hereby-formed, necessarily confused mass to a state of hopeless dilapidation. "This definition may be accepted provisionally."[1]

This was not a reassuring notice for the young instructor to receive, and it serves as a clue to some of the difficulties in his situation as a teacher. German philosophical idealism is unappealing stuff to most sensibilities, and Dewey's shy, sober presentation was not likely to sweeten it. Worse, the basic courses in the philosophy department were requirements in several of the curricula at Michigan, so many of the students in these classes were conscripts. For those with no taste for reflection it was doomed to be a bewildering experience, and they behaved accordingly. "In 1892 there turned up at the final examination of a class in Psychology three men in a row with Prof. Dewey's text-book open in their laps. They announced they were 'Company A, going through four abreast, Mr. So and So, Mr. So and So, Mr. So and So, and John Dewey.' "[2] What is remarkable is that even in these first few years Dewey had some success as a teacher, and not just with an occasional devotee. He seems to have gone on in his own imperturbable, high-minded way, utterly convinced of the importance of what he was teaching, and to have brought many of the better students more or less comprehendingly along with him. Charles Horton Cooley, the noted sociologist, captured it nicely:

> I had ... known him [Dewey] as a young instructor in the early eighties when I was an undergraduate. In the group to which I belonged his character was deeply admired, for its simplicity, perhaps, and for a fine gallantry, which, one felt sure, would never compromise the high purpose by which he was visibly animated. We believed that there was something highly original and significant in his philosophy, but had no definite idea as to what it was. [3]

Dewey did not remain so remote. He became more down to earth during the course of his career at Michigan. By his second five years there he was known as an advocate of more give-and-take in the classrooms and had involved himself increasingly in student extracurricular life. He had also found a special constituency within the student body, a group to whom his personal intellectual progress became very important. We catch a glimpse of it in a correspondence carried on in 1894 and 1895 between two upperclassmen, recent veterans of his classes. Frank Manny and Delos Wilcox were caught up in the most characteristic difficulty of their generation, the departure from orthodox Protestantism. Liberal religion, wrote Wilcox to his friend, is "Emerson or John Dewey or Henry Drummond or Geo. D. Herron," and he confesses he is torn between them and a more traditional personal devotion to "the Savior of the world." The events in the background of his letters are of the same cloth: a classmate has disappeared, leaving a note for his mother saying that she will never see him again, and later "is found a missionary in Australia, I hear"; Jessie Phelps, another classmate, has written a letter to Wilcox whose "chief topics" are "abstinence, purity, and self-culture or the care of one's person."[4] Fifty-five years later this Miss Phelps recalled in an interview: "I was doing some questioning of religion myself. Dewey evidently claimed to be a Christian, but he was certainly the most liberal one I had ever met. He never offended anyone in any way, but was able to help us think through certain problems." She concluded: "his influence helped me to rid myself of my old religious superstition and made me tolerant of all whom I met."[5]

Jessie Phelps and Delos Wilcox and Frank Manny were officers

of the Student Christian Association. Dewey was faculty adviser
to the organization, and he had helped them resist the edicts of
the reactionary national organization and counter the conserva-
tives within their own chapter. He was more than a tactical
adviser, however. As he had implied to William James, in his
May 1891 letter about his ethics classes ("Many of my students, I
find, are fairly hungering. They almost jump at any opportunity
to get out from under the load and to believe in their own lives"),
Dewey was developing a coherent liberal creed that would help
youngsters like Jessie Phelps and her friends see their way to
something they could live with. He presented it in his ethics
classes, in the occasional bible study groups he led, and in
addresses to the Student Christian Association. The evangelical
tone of his talks in his first years at Michigan ("The Obligation to
Knowledge of God," "Christ and Life," "The Place of Religious
Emotion") gave way in the nineties to the crisper parlance of
contemporary liberal Christianity, evident in titles such as
"Reconstruction," "The Relation of the Present Philosophic
Movement in Religious Thought," and "Christianity and Democracy."

Dewey delivered this last-mentioned address at the Sunday
Morning Services of the S.C.A. on 27 March 1892 (and
apparently showed Jane Addams a copy of it shortly afterward,
for when she wrote her famous essay "The Subjective Necessity
for Social Settlements" that summer, she borrowed her philosophical interpretation of Christianity from Dewey's text, in
large part verbatim). Despite its title, "Christianity and Democracy," the talk was as much or more about personal liberation:

> The condition of revelation is that it reveal. Christianity, if
> universal, if revelation, must be the continuously unfolding,
> never ceasing discovery of the meaning of life. It cannot be
> more than this; it must be all of this. Christianity then cannot
> stand or fall with any special theory or mode of action with
> which men at a given time may choose to identify it. Christian-
> ity in its reality knows no such exclusive or sectarian attitude.
> If it be made to stand or fall with any special theory, historical
> or ethical, if it be identified with some special act, ecclesiastic
> or ceremonial, it has denied its basis and its destiny. The one
> claim that Christianity makes is that God is truth; that as
> truth He is love and reveals Himself fully to man, keeping back
> nothing of himself; that man is so one with the truth thus

revealed that it is not so much revealed *to* him as *in* him; he is its incarnation; that by the appropriation of truth, by identification with it, man is free; free negatively, free from sin, free positively, free to live his own life, free to express himself, free to play without let or limitation upon the instrument given him—the environment of natural wants and forces. [6]

With theology such as this and with his sin-less ethics, Dewey was telling his students that he and they were the modern counterpart of Paul's early Christians: no longer under the law—free. Though we may have second thoughts about the optimism of such doctrine, Dewey was correct in his sense of what they needed to hear. In showing them a way through their late-adolescent crises, he was freeing them for the types of careers in matter-of-fact "scientific" social research and public service that were then appearing so rapidly in American institutional life. Cooley became a sociologist, Jessie Phelps an educator, Delos Wilcox a reforming publicist and administrator in municipal government, and Frank Manny a school official and collaborator with Dewey at the University of Chicago Laboratory School. Students of the American Progressive era will recognize the outlines of their story, for it was *the* story of that generation, repeated a thousand times, and told best in *Twenty Years at Hull House*, Jane Addams's wonderful recounting of her defeat of "subjectivity" by work for the commonweal.

ᛞ

While some of his students were finding their way to the social gospel and liberal Christianity through him, Dewey himself had already pushed beyond and was becoming self-consciously, even aggressively, a secular thinker. Along with secularization came politicization. At Michigan he began that record of liberalism on social and political issues that, along with the steadfast egalitarianism of his philosophy, would eventually earn him the sobriquet "philosopher of democracy."

It has been customary in an elegiac sort of way to attribute Dewey's pronounced democratic leanings to his origins as a Vermonter, the boy John Dewey being infected with democracy as by some Leveller miasma creeping on chilly nights up the streets of Burlington from Lake Champlain. But boyhood in Burlington can hardly have been an unambiguously democratic experience. The Yankees seem to have known who the "better people" were among themselves, and Burlington was also home to large numbers of Irish and French-Canadians, two working-class populations living apart in inferior neighborhoods. The people with whom the Deweys socialized, in the hilltop houses, had little to do with them. Nor would his father's politics account for Dewey's; Archibald Dewey's, it is safe to say, were dominated by the Civil War, Lincoln's crusading Republican Party, and the backdrop of the New England town. Not so his son's. For the origins of Dewey's political beliefs we should look to his experiences in graduate school and beyond. At Johns Hopkins, in such settings as the university's "Seminary of History and Politics," dedicated to "the application of historical and political science to American politics" and featuring, among its furniture, six bulletin boards labeled "International Politics," "American Politics," "Economic and Social Questions," "General History," "Ecclesiastical Matters," and "Book Notices, Education, University Affairs," Dewey received his first thorough exposure to an idea of politics that emphasized problems of modern government, international trade, cities, and immigration and that, moreover, was exploring the potential of research and professional expertise for solving these problems. As he listened to the presentations of fellow graduate students such as Woodrow Wilson, Dewey was participating, however unwittingly, in one of the first great marshalings of American Progressivism. [7]

Dewey did not leave Johns Hopkins a political thinker. He was a metaphysician and philosophical psychologist. But he had been exposed to "advanced thinking" on matters social and political and would continue to encounter it at Michigan. One of Dewey's earliest and best friends there was Henry Carter Adams, another Johns Hopkins Ph.D., a man already in trouble for his "radical" views, including a suspect attitude toward the institution of private property, advocacy of free trade, and sympathy for the Knights of Labor. It is Carter's touch we see when, in 1888, in a talk "The Ethics of Democracy," Dewey insisted that "there is no need to beat about the bush in saying that democracy is not in reality what it is in name until it is industrial, as well as civil and political ...; a democracy of wealth is a necessity."[8]

Alice Dewey, the woman Dewey married, exercised a similar influence on him. Her grandfather, one Fred Riggs, with whom she and Dewey spent a good deal of time, was the "village atheist" of Fenton, Michigan, and, as a rare champion of Indian rights, had become an adopted son of the Chippewa tribe. Alice herself was something of a feminist and was by all accounts an unusual woman.[9] There survives in the letters of a friend of the Deweys' a little vignette that tells much about her. In 1893 Henry Northrup Castle, a close friend of Dewey's colleague George Herbert Mead, visited Ann Arbor and, after staying some months, traveled to Germany, leaving his wife, Mabel, and three-year-old daughter in the care of the Meads and Deweys. Alice Chipman Dewey—or rather Mabel's reactions to her—is very much at the center of the chatty letters Mabel sent to her husband during those months. On New Year's Eve, 1893, she wrote to Henry:

> Last night Mrs. Dewey and I sat before the open fire two hours discussing vital issues, and among other things she gave me a talk on Zola—his scope, his scheme, his success. . . . Our progeny disport mildly or wildly as we chat or read by day, but at night we have an opportunity to become a bit better acquainted with each other. My admiration for her is unbounded, and I am delighted to find that mama shares in it. I believe that Mrs. Dewey does look at things frankly, with the utmost honesty, the utmost reason and understanding I have yet seen in a woman—of men I say nothing. I enjoy Mrs. Dewey, and she helps me to think of life, real activities, more than the subjectivities of my own communings with self.[10]

Mabel repeated these sentiments on other occasions; "Mrs. Dewey's able to speak with authority on so many things," she exclaimed in a letter to her husband's parents.[11] And yet her response was not unambiguous: she was catty about the rough-and-ready manners of the young Dewey children; when Alice kissed her as she was leaving one afternoon, Mabel confessed her surprise to her husband, "for I had thought of her as rather out of anything of the kind."[12] Indeed, there was a pattern, at most half-conscious, in her letters of ascribing to Alice Dewey masculine virtues and of attributing to herself, by contrast, the characteristics of "femininity"—refinement, sentimentality, delicacy, vagueness. In her letters Alice is the aggressor, the propounder; herself, the passive receiver. Part, at least, of this pattern is not entirely an idiosyncrasy of Mabel's; as one reads through fragments of correspondence that survive from the academic community around the Deweys in Ann Arbor in the 1880s and 1890s, one is reminded again and again of the prevalence of neurasthenic symptoms among women of the middle and upper classes in late-nineteenth-century America. "At some periods," wrote one young matron in the group to her mother, "I feel my constant depression is the result of the climate, for my nerves are unable to endure this unspeakably trying climate. We have made up our minds to give it up, and use every effort to spend our summers abroad—on the French or English coasts. We both feel that Charlevoix [a Michigan resort town] with its magnificent lake breezes and water life is overstimulating." [13]

Alice Dewey was a different sort altogether, and Dewey was a lucky man and seems to have known it. Indeed, the testimony of the men on the subject of Mrs. Dewey was altogether unambiguous: "Mrs. D. I found more charming than ever," Henry Castle found when he returned from Germany. "She is one of the most refreshing persons I have come in contact with. A mind rich and varied—with a wide experience—and finding the world constantly entertaining and interesting." [14] In the sketch of his life published in 1939, twelve years after Alice's death, Dewey had his daughter write,

> Awakened by her grandparents to a critical attitude toward social conditions and injustices, she was undoubtedly largely responsible for the early widening of Dewey's philosophic interests from the commentative and classical to the field of contemporary life. Above all, things which had previously been matters of theory acquired through his contact with her a vital and direct human significance. [15]

∞

These various experiences paved the way for Dewey's first grand venture into politics, the *Thought News* episode. The man who led him into it was a Franklin Ford, one of those persons who surface momentarily in history, coming seemingly from nowhere and then disappearing without a trace. [16] We know that

Ford was an editor of *Bradstreet's* commercial newspaper in New York in the early 1880s; and, as he told the story later, he had come to the conviction that *Bradstreet's* and *Dun's*, its competitor, were doing little more than reporting financial gossip and letting space to advertisers. One day in 1883 there had come across Ford's desk a letter from a man who was considering investing in a new railroad to be built in one of the western states. The man wanted to know the agricultural prospects of that part of the farm belt. Ford found that, with only a few staff reporters and the usual "sources" available to a fairly small newspaper, he had no systematic way of finding out such information. The only way the letter-writer could get the information he wanted would be to commission personally a thorough investigation of the subject—a prohibitively expensive prospect.

Ford conceived of an alternative way of doing things. Why not, he urged the management of the Bradstreet Company, set up an association of experts, a national bureau of information, whose business it would be to initiate research of their own and, for a fee, undertake investigations for potential investors? *Bradstreet's* rejected Ford's suggestions, and he quit their paper. Franklin Ford's basic idea has of course long since been implemented under one or another set of auspices; one thinks of the work of government research bureaus (in part already in existence in Ford's time), of contract research in the universities, of newspaper reports-in-depth, and so forth. It is the same with the other journalistic reforms he began to ask for: less subservience to the interests of advertisers, clear separation of editorializing from reporting, and less emphasis on sensational events and more on underlying processes.

But this is not all there was to Ford. Right from the start there appears to have been an eccentric and star-crossed side to his ideas. Certainly, by the time he printed them up in a pamphlet, "Draft of Action," in 1893, their basic mechanics had become a grandiose scheme, and the modern reader is reminded at once that he is looking at a relic of the second great age of American utopianism, the 1880s and 1890s of Edward Bellamy's *Looking Backward* and a hundred other utopian novels, the time of the Henry George clubs and the flowering of countless such one-shot solutions to the ills of a country panicked by its too rapid transformation. In his "Draft of Action" Ford presented "The

Intelligence Triangle," a scheme for a vast central clearinghouse of information—*all* the information, about *everything*—in America. The clearinghouse was to have three organs: "Ford's," a purified version of *Bradstreet's* ("Ford's is the Lloyd's of information; it is the universal truth-shop." "BUY YOUR FACTS AT FORD's. Corporations investigated. Trade conditions reported."); second, the Class News Company, putting out as many newspapers as there were special interests and industries in the country (papers with names like "Meat" and "Fruit" and "Cotton"); and third, the News Association, issuing *Newsbook* (a national political and commercial paper), regional and local newspapers *ad libitum*, and newspapers given exclusively to classified advertising ("The Daily Want"). Obviously, somewhere along the line Ford had become a syndicalist (he pauses in his sketching, it should be said, to denounce Rockefeller as a parasite and to hail his workers as the true industrialists), and his giant intelligence-gathering and intelligence-distributing apparatus was meant to be the instrument that would bring about an orderly and just society. As he concluded grandly, at the end of one of his little chapters, "We are able to see how through becoming the receiver and transmitter of the price-making fact the journalist gains the central position in life. Industry is at last organized because the intelligence peculiar thereto has become organic to the whole." [17]

This latter esoteric pronouncement—industry "at last organized because the intelligence peculiar thereto has become organic to the whole"—can be made to serve as an introduction to a further level of theory and rhetoric, more totalist and arcane than any mere syndicalism, which sweeps through Franklin Ford's 1893 "Draft of Action." It was a language that he and John Dewey had brewed up together.

After his great discovery at the desk of *Bradstreet's* in 1883, Ford spent several years in New York City trying to convert the managers of its newspapers to his plans. It proved to be unrewarding work. So did his attempts to gain support from rank-and-file reporters and editors and his proselytizing trip in 1887—a journey, as he described it, through "all the news centers of the country east of the Rocky Mountains." Finally, in 1888, Ford's groping for a foothold brought him to the universities. He spent four months touring the philosophy, history, and infant social science faculties at Columbia, Harvard, Yale, Cornell, Johns

Hopkins, Pennsylvania, and Michigan, looking for "a man and men who would give more than a passive assent to the principle. In this I succeeded at the University of Michigan. I got to John Dewey." [18]

Get to him he did. Dewey had a lifelong weakness for quacks. It was a foible, but it also told something about his convictions and character. He would always be uneasy about the pro-fessionalization of philosophy and its progressive confinement to academia. He wanted it to be a public thing and an activity of everyman. There was little he could do in a programmatic way to bring this about; but when the amateurs, irregulars, or holy fools approached him, out of principle he gave them an audience. This gave him some trying moments, but fortunately he had the temperament that could tolerate them; he really was a democrat.

When Franklin Ford came to Ann Arbor, or, more likely, when he found he had a reception there, he brought along one of his brothers, Corydon, an even stranger, pricklier eccentric than Franklin. In his autobiography, *The Child of Democracy*, written in 1894, Corydon Ford indicated in his remarkable prose what he and his brother saw in Dewey:

> . . . he was searching for the State when my brother and I found him. . . . In Professor Dewey we found the sympathy of an intelligent cooperation with the ideas of an advance in letters which we had brought from the field of a practice— the laboratory of the moving fact in the region of the school and the newspaper. The reality of our waiting at the gates of the University was to find the last fact bearing on the advance of our practice. He pointed us to the construction of the books in what bore upon it. Through his condensations of an exhaustive reading in penetration of newness he brought up for us the past in such economy that our movement was little checked. He gave us the books as of surviving things in his spent research of the old ideas. He stood for us as the great central archive in the State, had in such order that it could be connected with the advance or moving fact. He made for the mobile science on the side of the State, being for us the scientist of the Whole, the philosopher. [19]

It is a pity that we have no way of recreating any of the numerous sessions that Franklin Ford and Dewey had with each other in that spring of 1888 and over the following four years, for they seem to have been marvelously exciting: Ford on one side of the desk, spinning out his notion of society and his newspaper schemes, Dewey on the other, declaring, "Yes, I see what you mean! What you mean is this, isn't it?", and Ford, after years out in the cold, hearing his beloved plans coming back across the desk to him, somewhat transfigured but grandly put—and by a professor! What it finally brought Dewey to was a comic misadventure, but a revealing one.

It is clear from the episode that Dewey had been chafing at the distance of his discipline from the main action in American political life. He was a Hegelian, after all, and Hegel was a political philosopher. Like a good many Americans with German notions in their heads, Dewey was tantalized by the idea of an ordered social organism and frustrated by its remoteness from the American political reality. Nevertheless, had Franklin Ford not happened along, Dewey's political activity in the 1880s and 1890s would probably have been limited to expressing reformist sympathies, voting Democratic, and associating with such projects as Hull House—in brief, what we have come to recognize as the normal fate of American academic liberals. But in Ford Dewey thought he saw a chance to do more. He immediately began to make the same unwarranted leap in reasoning that Ford had. That is to say, instead of seeing Ford's array of proposed journals as simply one way of dissecting national life so as to get a better look at it, he put on syndicalist glasses and saw Ford's classification as *the* biology of society.

He began with some caution. In 1889 he explained Ford's scheme to Henry Carter Adams by saying that "the state of things falls naturally into a number of subdivisions";[20] but within a year or two, in the extraordinary dialect he and Ford were concocting, Ford was referring to society as an "achieved organism," and Dewey himself was saying that the troubles of the nation were to be blamed on the "state of intelligence on its thought side." Ford had given Dewey such a vivid dramatization of the workings of the economy, of the wondrous trystings of supply and demand, of production, distribution, and consumption, and had described so affectingly the failure of economic newsgathering to keep up with these processes and to facilitate them (he pictured grain rotting on a siding in Iowa because a would-be buyer in New York didn't know it was there), that Dewey concluded it was principally a deficit of intelligence that stood between America and the good society. "Intelligence," that is, "news," was Ford's, the reporter's business; but after all, wasn't "intelligence," that is "mind," his own, Dewey's, business? He was entranced.

Ford convinced Dewey that the time was ripe; information, "intelligence," should now become universally and instantaneously available, for distance had been eliminated by the twin inventions, the "loco-motive" and the "tele-graph."[21] Dewey, it goes without saying, subscribed almost unconsciously to the characteristic fallacy of the Progressive generation that scientific knowledge and an informed public were essentially all that was needed for curing America's ills. As he explained in the memorandum he sent Adams:

> That which finally touches everybody is the public thing— politics—the state of the social organism. The newspaper in giving publicity to public matters (not for reform, or for any other purpose excepting that it is its business to sell facts) becomes the representative of public interests. Thus Ford says the municipal question is essentially a publicity question. No paper can afford now to tell the truth about the actual conduct of the city's business. But have a newspaper whose *business*, i.e. whose livelihood, was to sell intelligence, and it couldn't afford to do anything else, any more than any genuine business can afford to sell spurious goods. [22]

For the rest, once the communications problems were cleared up, good government was inevitable, along with surcease from our economic problems. The cornucopia of supply and demand was poised, ready to pour out its bounty. "It only needs reporting," said Dewey.

Nor would he be satisfied by anything less than reading all this back into philosophy. Wasn't it Hegel come true? Wasn't society as Ford elucidated it the social organism that Hegel thought he saw, and *now*, in view of this culmination as an "achieved organism," didn't history make sense after all? Dewey mulled and puzzled over Ford's meanings and implications for three years and then, in 1891, prepared to throw aside the caution of a closet utopian and proclaim publicly that these were world-historic times. In an article he wrote early that year for Paul Carus's journal, the *Monist*, he took up the charge that for Hegel thought meant "thought in the old, scholastic sense, a process apart and fixed in itself, and yet somehow evolving truth out of its own inner being, out of its own enclosed ruminations." It was a false charge, said Dewey, and a particularly damaging one in an empirical and scientific age. Hegel had been trying to say just the opposite. "He denies not only the possibility of getting truth out of a formal, apart thought, but he denies the existence of any faculty of thought which is other than the expression of fact itself. His contention is not that 'thought,' in the scholastic sense, has ontological validity, but that fact, reality is significant." The universe is not "a mere hodgepodge of fragments" but a systematic, organic whole, and, the whole once grasped, every fact is seen to have a place and its meaning in terms of it. [23]

Hegel had come to seem "transcendental" and unreal to late-nineteenth-century scientists and intellectuals, Dewey argued, because he had had to outline reality fifty or seventy-five years before the time was ripe:

> . . . the rationality of fact had not been sufficiently realized in detail in the early years of the century to admit of the principle of the "transcendental" movement being other than misunderstood. That is to say, the development of science and, more particularly, its application to the specific facts of the world was comparatively rudimentary. . . . The difficulties in the way of conceiving a world upon which science had not expended its energies in detail, as an organism of significant relations and bearings were so great that Hegel's attempt to point out these significant types and functions as immanent in reality was inevitably misconstrued as an attempt, on Hegel's part, to prove that a system of purely "subjective" thoughts could somehow be manipulated to give objectively valid results. [24]

But now, in 1891, we must rephrase it and ask Hegel's question again. "Has the application of scientific thought to the world of fact gone far enough so that we can speak, without seeming strained, of the rationality of fact?"

> When we speak of the rationality, of the intrinsic meaning of fact, can these terms be understood in their direct and obvious sense, and not in any remote, or *merely* metaphysical sense? Has the theoretical consideration of fact in its detailed study, has practical invention, as the manifestation of the rationality of fact, gone far enough so that this significance

has become, or could become with some effort, as real and objective a material of study as are molecules and vibrations? [25]

"It seems to me," Dewey answered, "that we are already at this stage, or are at the point of getting to it." In June he gave the commencement speech at Smith College. His theme was the disparity between the agnosticism of contemporary philosophy and the hopefulness and faith of poetry—"an unnatural divorce of the spirit":

[This divorce] exists and endures, not because of a glow to life which philosophy cannot catch, nor because of a verifiable truth which poetry cannot detect and convey. It exists because in the last few centuries the onward movement of life, of experience, has been so rapid, its diversification of regions and methods so wide, that it has outrun the slower step of reflective thought. Philosophy has not as yet caught the rhythmic swing of this onward movement, and written it down in a score of black and white which all may read. Or if in some degree philosophy has laid hold of the secret of this movement, it has not yet been able to tell it in straightforward, simple syllables to the common consciousness. [26]

Again, as in "The Present Position of Logical Theory," Dewey was bursting to tell his audience that he had in his hands the means to fulfill the promise of the age. But, as he had remarked in his article, there was no point in *saying* it; his claim could "be proved only by acting on it, only *ambulando*."[27] He and Ford would commence the revelation of the meaning of the age straightaway. Their vehicle would be a newspaper, *Thought News*, "a journal of inquiry and a record of fact."[28]

Ford and Dewey appear to have worked on the plans for their paper all that fall and winter, and Dewey's actual scholarly output dropped off to almost nothing. His prose had already taken on a most uncharacteristic Fordian swagger (his piece on logical theory had him conjuring up the threats posed to the "modern *Zeitgeist*" by "the cohorts of the army of external authority" and remarking that no one any longer took the study of formal logic very seriously—"unless here and there some belated 'professor' "),[29] but now his writing fairly crackled with impatience. One of the few things he wrote for publication that fall was a contribution to the *Inlander*, a Michigan student magazine of which he was moderator. "The Scholastic and the Speculator" he called it, and his villain was "the scholastic," a medieval creature originally, but, unhappily, reborn.[30]

> The monastic cell has become a professional lecture hall; an endless mass of "authorities" have taken the place of Aristotle. *Jahresberichte*, monographs, journals without end occupy the void left by the commentators upon Aristotle. If the older Scholastic spent his laborious time in erasing the writing from old manuscripts in order to indite thereon something of his own, the new Scholastic has also his palimpsest. He criticises the criticisms with which some other Scholastic has criticised other criticisms, and the writing upon writings goes on till the substructure of reality is long obscured.[31]

What the times demand is the opposite: "intelligence must throw its fund out again into the stress of life; it must venture its savings against the pressure of facts." We need the speculator. "All the great philosophers have had something of this ruthless adventure of thought, this reckless throwing of the accumulated store of truth. ... Action upon truth marks the merchant of thought, who, though he both saves and spends, yet neither embezzles nor gambles."

Dewey was doing such thundering in part to summon up his own courage. Early in March 1892, as the publication date for the first issue of the journal bore down on him, he wrote to James Rowland Angell, a young former student of his, about his dreams for philosophy and action. His letter concluded, "These things would sound more or less crazy to a professor of philosophy in good and regular standing, but I intend henceforth to act on my conviction regardless. Hence, among other things, *Thought News*."[32] Two weeks earlier, on February 27, Dewey had sent Angell an advance copy of the circular announcing *Thought News* and had remarked somewhat nervously that the plans were "not quite mature yet" and that he was for the moment holding back on distribution of the circulars. On March 8, he edged a bit deeper into the water and sent a circular to Thomas Davidson. (Davidson, it is worth noticing, though a distinguished philosopher, was himself not "a professor of philosophy in good and regular standing"; he was a self-supporting itinerant, one of the last philosophers attached to no university.) Even with Davidson,

Dewey dissembled the extent of his personal investment in *Thought News*, calling it simply "a project, with which I shall while away my leisure hours."[33] The circular was finally released for publication in the March 16 student newspaper, the *Michigan Daily*:

In April next will appear the first number of the "Thought News." This will be a newspaper and will aim to perform the function of a newspaper. The world is already supplied, if not burdened, with magazines of philosophy, theology, literature and political science. It is believed there is room, in the flood of opinion, for one journal which shall not go beyond the fact; which shall report thought rather than dress it up in the garments of the past; which instead of dwelling at length upon the merely individual processes that accompany the facts, shall set forth the facts themselves; which shall not discuss philosophic ideas per se but use them as tools in interpreting the movements of thought; which shall treat questions of science, letters, state, school and church as parts of the one moving life of man and hence common interest, and not relegate them to separate documents of merely technical interest; which shall report new investigations and discoveries in their net outcome instead of in their overloaded gross bulk; which shall note new contributions to thought, whether by book or magazine, from the standpoint of the news in them, and not from that of patron or censor.

"Thought News" will aim to be of the size of the news it has to deliver and to appear as often as the material at hand warrants, neither swelling its reports for the sake of paper and ink, nor withholding news out of respect to a given day of the month. It will appear, however, at least once a month. It will be a quarto and contain from twelve to sixteen pages. The subscription price will be $1.50 per volume—twelve issues to the volume. The immediate responsibility for its conduct will be in the hands of John Dewey of the philosophical department of the University of Michigan.

The need of the paper lies in the present condition of intelligence on the thought side. The enterprise is prompted by an inquiry movement centering in Ann Arbor.

Address all communications to The Thought News, Ann Arbor, Michigan.

The chance reader of the *Michigan Daily* might have noticed that in several specifics (a journal "which shall report thought

rather than dress it up in the garments of the past; which instead
of dwelling at length upon the merely individual processes that
accompany the facts, shall set forth the facts themselves . . . the
present condition of intelligence on its thought side . . .") the
author was evidently speaking from a frame of reference that he
was not sharing completely with his readers, but other than that
he would not have found Dewey's release an especially remarkable or portentous manifesto. The radical metaphysical and
social premises that lay behind it were not in evidence. Alas for
Dewey, the same could not be said for the release that appeared
three weeks later in the *Michigan Daily* of April 8, announcing
April 22 as the publication date for the first issue of *Thought
News*. Though the accompanying statement was not signed, it is
clear from its content that its author was the uninhibited
Franklin Ford:

> On or about April 22 there will issue from the press in this
> city a new paper, *Thought News*, conducted by John Dewey of
> the philosophical department of the university. The date will
> mark the first appearance in visible merchantable printed
> types of a new idea in journalism and education. . . .
> Mr. Dewey calls the paper "A Report of the Social Fact."
> The social fact is the social organism. Properly, *Thought News*
> has but one thing to report and that is a mere announcement—
> the announcement that the social organism is here.
>
> A report is more than a mere statement. The statement
> that society is an organism was made long ago and accepted—
> as a statement. It remains now to point to the fact, the visible,
> tangible thing, to show the idea in motion. If the social organ-
> ism is a fact and not a poetic dream it must be studied
> like a steam engine, in its principle, but also in its practical
> activity. In order that the social organism may be understood,
> it is necessary to see the idea in motion—it is necessary to
> report it, that is, describe it as it moves in life. That is what
> *Thought News* will attempt to do. It will report society in
> order that it may be seen to be an idea in motion. It will
> report it for thought.
>
> There is the new idea in journalism and in education. On the
> one hand the newspaper is to apply the historical method to the
> reporting of everyday life—to report not the happening, but
> the fact, the typical fact, the fact which illustrates the
> principle. On the other hand if the student is to get his facts at
> first hand, he is to apply his principles to life, he is to report.

The newspaper is to report not a divorce, but divorce; the student is to study not books on municipal government, not charters and the laws, but "boodle."

In this the reporter, the fact man, becomes scientific and the student, the theory man, becomes the reporter. So the chasm between education and real life, between theory and practice, is bridged over once and forever.

If Dewey in all his native diffidence was aghast when he put down the April 8 edition of the *Michigan Daily*, he would have done well to keep in reserve some of his capacity for horror, for the worst was yet to come. The *Detroit Tribune* had a correspondent in Ann Arbor, and on April 10 his weekly dispatch appeared, a long two columns devoted almost entirely to Dewey, describing the mounting excitement at the university as the community awaited the first issue of *Thought News*, and reprinting Ford's release in its entirety. The correspondent allowed himself a few comments on the enterprise. "Just how Mr. Dewey is to report thought no one seems to exactly understand, and Mr. Dewey has not yet explained. . . . It is generally understood from this [the circular] that Mr. Dewey proposes to get out an 'extra' everytime he has a new thought—in that case the subscribers will be largely dependent upon the stability of Mr. Dewey's digestion for their news." Relentless, the reporter then turned his attention to Dewey's other activity on campus:

There is every evidence that the new philosophy which Professor Dewey teaches has taken an immense hold upon the students of the University. It has become the fad now to talk in the jargon of psychology. It may not be as forcible as the ordinary speech but it is much more scientific and at times a great deal more delicate, as for instance when a psychological student wishes to call attention to his neighbor's conceit he says, mildly, that he is "too subjective" or if he wishes to say a man has the "blues" he says he is "reacting upon himself." A writer in the University of Michigan *Daily* the other day advised the class of '93 to attend the class sociable at Newberry Hall in order that "they might assemble together and realize their individuality."[34]

The following morning, Monday, saw a lead editorial, no less, in the *Detroit Tribune* replying indignantly to the criticisms of ordinary newspapers implied in Ford's description of *Thought*

News. (The editors attributed it all to Dewey.) Tuesday brought a *Tribune* correspondent to Dewey's office. Dewey took the interview as his chance to backpedal. "The matter to which *The Tribune* refers," he said carefully, "must have been someone's conception of what *Thought News* is to be. It wasn't given out by me." He continued:

> *Thought News* hasn't such ambitious designs as *The Tribune* editorial credits it with. Its object is not to introduce a new idea into journalism at large, but to show that philosophy has some use. You know Mr. Huxley once called philosophy a matter of lunar politics—it was all remote and abstract. That's about the way it strikes the student, and the difficulty is to show him that there is some fact to which philosophic ideas refer. That fact is the social organism. When philosophic ideas are not inculcated by themselves but used as tools to point out the meaning of phases of social life they begin to have some life and value. Instead of trying to change the newspaper business by introducing philosophy into it, the idea is to transform philosophy somewhat by introducing a little newspaper business into it. When it can be seen for example, that Walt Whitman's poetry, the great development of short stories at present, the centralizing tendency in the railroads and the introduction of business methods into charity organizations are all parts of one organic social movement, then the philosophic ideas about organism begin to look like something definite. The facts themselves get more meaning, too, when viewed with relation to one principle than when treated separately as a jumble. This is what the writer meant, probably, when he alluded to the difference between "happenings" and "typical facts." Any happening, however slight, is typical, if treated as an expression of some law, of the movement of a whole. Any fact, however big, is only an accident if not treated as a symptom, as an exponent. It is quite possible that the daily newspaper treats events more as accidents than typical. It must do so until it gets hold of the social law, but that's not the affair, one way or the other, of *Thought News*.[35]

The article had for its headline "He's Planned No Revolution," an appropriate title indeed for the modest purposes Dewey expressed to the reporter. Yet it must be said that it was exactly "a revolution" that Dewey had been intending when he committed

himself to the *Thought News* project. He had been sidling into it
until Ford made his great brag to the press. The sudden public
light which this threw on the venture seems finally to have
broken Ford's spell over his professor-collaborator and to have
made Dewey acknowledge that Ford was a very peculiar
character indeed.

Ford, we may imagine, saw Dewey's interview for what it was.
The professor's session with the press was surely followed by a
more painful session with Ford himself. On April 18, the *Detroit
Tribune* had some more fun at their expense, proposing the
interest of University of Michigan male students in Ypsilanti
factory girls as a mystery within the social organism that *Thought
News* ought to attempt to solve. As late as April 20, the editors at
the Ann Arbor *Courier* were still expecting that *Thought News*
would be printed in the *Courier's* offices. On April 23, Dewey
sent a business note to Thomas Davidson about the Deweys'
summer cabin in the Adirondacks. Mrs. Dewey, he mentioned,
had just left on a sudden trip to the Hawaiian Islands. He made
no mention of *Thought News*. On April 25 he wrote to James
Angell. The letter noted simply, "We have postponed publication
of *Thought News* for the present; will take it up later on a larger
scale and with more adequate financial outfit," and then turned
to other matters. Apparently no public announcement of the
postponement was made, for on April 27 *Thought News* received
its last public notice in the form of a grumbling remark on the
editorial page of the *Washtenaw* [Michigan] *Evening Times*:

> The new publication "Thought News" was announced to
> appear April 22. If it does not appear closer to the announced
> day after it is once started the absence of a subscription list is
> likely to produce deep thought in its financial backers.

Years later, Dewey remembered, "No issue was made: it was an
overenthusiastic project which we had not the means nor the time
to carry through. . . . The *idea* was advanced for those days, but
it was too advanced for the maturity of those who had the idea in
mind."[36]

There survives no trace of any last transactions between Dewey
and Franklin Ford. Ford surfaced for a moment five years later in
New York City, still trying to get someone important to listen,
and then he seems to disappear again. It was left to his brother,

Corydon, to exact what poor revenge the Fords had on Dewey. In his autobiography, *The Child of Democracy*, published two years later in 1894, he told why Dewey, for all his promise, failed him and his brother Franklin:

> . . . denied any direct demand from the State, he could not put the new ideas on life. He could not give the Supreme Court at Lansing the revolution of its concept or Detroit the remedy for the disorder of its city government; he could not put the cross upon President Angell who stood against progress upon the Campus; neither might he denounce as a Judas his earnest pastor falsifying Christ. Clogged of the dead institution, he could not move; his salary meant that he was to keep quiet as to the overturning concepts. He must either forego his bribe and become the tramp upon the highway that he might have voice; or he could remain to take the sop of convention and upstew the old ideas with the new as the made-dish of apart theory. [37]

Corydon Ford then turned his attention to Professor Fred Newton Scott—who had collaborated with Dewey and the Fords and had initiated the country's first course in journalism in the university's Department of English in 1891—and accused him (and the other professors) of stealing the Fords' ideas. The contrary was true. It was Corydon who had set about publishing other people's ideas—John Dewey's, to be specific. He had attended Dewey's Course 5 in the philosophy department, "Introduction to Philosophy," taken copious notes, added fifteen pages of his own ramblings at the end, copyrighted the sixty-page package, and published it in 1893 under the title, *The Synthesis of Mind: The Method of a Working Psychology by Corydon Ford. 1883–1893.* Similarly, he used Dewey's ideas and language to describe his own experiences as a rural schoolmaster in the late 1880s. Poor Ford's plagiarisms got him nowhere, but they do help us to appreciate Dewey. As he taught it in the year that Corydon Ford attended it, Dewey's Course 5, "Introduction to Philosophy," was an important document in his progress as a thinker. There has survived an outline of the course, put together and printed up by Dewey, and Ford's notes flesh it out nicely. [38]

The same thing is true for Dewey's ideas on pedagogy at this time, still five years or so before he founded the famous University of Chicago Laboratory School. Dewey had had little to say about education in print, the longest indication of what he was thinking being a paragraph at the end of an article in 1891, "How Do Concepts Arise from Percepts?" "It is evident that there is but one genuine way to lead the mind of the pupil on from percept to concept: to present, from the first, the percept in its genesis, in its origin and growth, in its proper relations. . . . Let the object be, as it were, *done* over and over again."[39] These few remarks are supplemented by material in Corydon's 1894 autobiography and in a pamphlet he wrote in 1891 with a similar title. He describes in a sort of parody of what we would recognize as Dewey's language his adventures in helping slow or bored grade-school children, and he gives us our first glimpse, if badly distorted, of the Lab School itself:

> . . . the child must be organized for an apprenticeship to the daily avocations of the State. . . . This would make the organic connection with life, and in the fulness of his function the child would be born into independence of affairs. Through the placenta of an organized contact with industry, through practice in responsibility, the child would be fed of his need. Torn no longer of the unreal and apart thing, he would rather be distributed to such doing as he could and the paths of employment organized as open to his progress: the foundry, the loom, the plough, chemistry, journalism. The child would come to such a place as that in which I worked, for purposes of specific drill as the requirements of his daily avocation made the need. The only parallel to life was life itself. This was the school.[40]

In general, it is clear from Ford's scribblings that in 1890, and 1891, and 1892, Dewey and his intimates spent a good deal of time talking about the failures of primary education, that they mulled over the programs of such reformers as Pestalozzi and Francis Parker, and that their own ideas had begun to take a shape that we can today recognize as Deweyan.

တ

One of the questions that follow false starts is How could they have been avoided? Dewey had personal characteristics that made him a potential participant in such misadventures, and that helps to account for his getting into this particular one. There was a clue to more of the answer in one of the subordinate themes of the *Thought News* mobilization. One advertisement for the paper went:

If you are studying by yourself,
If you are interested in the application of ideas to life,
If you are interested in the application of theory to practice,
You will be interested
in
Thought News. [41]

And in his apologetic interview with the *Detroit Tribune* correspondent, Dewey remarked, "there are lots of persons around the country who are scientifically interested in the study of social questions. Not having any definite direction, they are reading in an indefinite way in the books or else they are tangled up with some general theory like Bellamy's. ... These students might investigate questions at first hand in their own towns."[42]

The manifest theme of these items in the *Inlander* and the *Detroit Tribune* is social theory and investigation, but more intriguing is the implied sociology of this would-be intelligentsia: they are seen as scattered, isolated people. This was in part a projection of the Fords' personal experiences, but there was more to it. Isolation marked the lives of most of the men we encounter in this book: George Sylvester Morris in his most difficult years at Michigan, G. Stanley Hall at Antioch taking the train to Saint Louis to find some people to talk to, Dewey in Oil City. The fact hardly needs dramatizing; it might be more useful to compare the situations of these American Victorians with that of the main body of Victorian intellectuals, their English contemporaries. We have been graced with a fabulous legacy of English Victorian memoirs, autobiographies, and, subsequently, biographies. To read them, especially to read them from an American perspective, is to be struck by the richness and density of the social-intellectual life led by the young mid- and late-Victorian contemporaries of George Morris and John Dewey. For some, such as Leslie Stephen and Beatrice Potter Webb, it was a family or group of families with wealth, a place of importance in English public life, and a tradition of involvement in civic and religious matters that propelled the children from their early years into a world of ideas and of company in ideas. For others, such as Morris's model, Thomas Hill Green, it was the elite secondary schools and one or the other of the two great universities, Oxford and Cambridge, institutions with a profoundly centralizing and intensifying effect on English intellectual life. The list of such English conditions could be extended almost indefinitely: physically a small country (putting people of like mind in close proximity to each other), home of a vast empire, it was possessed of a comparatively large leisure class, a quite large and distinguished civil service and legal profession, and a government highly centralized in London, along with Crown, court, and "society." The last two, court and society, were to Beatrice Webb's mind scandalously open to new wealth, new style, and sudden genius. This may indeed have given London circles a vulgarity, but by the same token it made the city hospitable to provincial or unsponsored talent. Like so many of these other elements, it tended to weave the country's intellectual life into a close, variegated, brilliant cloth.

The effect of all this shows through in Victorian biography; the number of other notables whom any one figure is likely to know is breathtaking. Nor was it simply like gathering to like—writers to writers, artists to artists—for capitalists, men of letters, government figures, the titled, the wealthy, philanthropists, reformers, and even (though perhaps less frequently) dons knew one another through family, politics, religion, Oxford, Cambridge, and London. Such life was undemocratic, imperial, elitist, and usually appallingly remote from the poor and the common people of England, but, that said, it must be added that it stood in enviable contrast to the situation in America. Point by point, the contrast holds: the United States was a vast country with decentralized political power and wealth, an undistinguished life in its national capital and a small federal civil service, and—most immediate and important for men like Dewey and the others—its colleges and universities were scattered across three thousand miles, far from one another, far from any national center, and even within their own states and regions usually situated in rural towns removed from local centers of power and government. (Dewey and Ford proposed to move the University of Michigan from Ann Arbor to Detroit or, failing that, to tie the university to the city by telegraph and telephone.)

The richness of the intellectual milieu in England and its comparative barrenness in most of America affected the thought of the two countries in numerous ways, many of them obvious. The ways in which the situation was reflected in young Dewey's thought are not quite obvious, but the characteristics in question are important to the tone of his thought. Earlier, at the end of chapter 4, I suggested that William James's "pluralistic universe" and Dewey's inability to see the world that way were somehow related to the cosmopolitanism of the one man and the provinciality of the other. James was from the one small group of people in the United States who could claim most convincingly to be an exception to the generalization made above about Victorian America: the Boston circle that included in its number his brother Henry, Oliver Wendell Holmes, Jr., and Henry Adams. Their setting was a city; the city itself and their families or the families of their friends had been important, even central, for some generations in the commercial, political, and cultural life of the nation. Harvard was there. Added to this, in the case of the Jameses, were the peculiarities of their upbringing: a childhood of almost incessant travel and of schooling in the major capitals of Europe, and a father who cultivated religious eclecticism in his children. How different, this, from Dewey's town boyhood and religious rearing, with its rigorous expectation of coherency in matters of belief.

The contrast continues. Urbanity meant encounter with diversity. Henry Adams's great autobiography (set almost completely in cities—London, Boston, Washington) recounts his jarring encounters with diversity—"multiplicity" was the expression he used—and with a world that had become too variegated to answer to any simple system of it. As he told it in *The Education*, his life became a search for a law that could make this world thinkable by finite human intelligence. What is most to be noted for our purposes is not his search but the series of devices he developed to enable him to cope in the meantime with this apparently irreducible multiplicity: irony, skepticism, intellectual reserve, personal detachment, stoicism. How different this, and how different the Jameses' cultivated openness to the *outré*, the urbane sophistication they wore as a birthright, from the simplicity, the moral and intellectual earnestness, the directness and optimism of Dewey. Could it be that in these early years

Dewey had never so much as dreamt of the world of apparently infinite variation that travelers and cosmopolitans like James and Adams had already experienced? That his imagination had been formed by finitude, by town and town church, and that his philosophy was certain to have analogous features? Henry Adams claimed that he was disabled by the multiplicity of his experiences, each with its shock and mystery, each implying its own world, each world different. Henry James's prose, in answering to the complexity and nuance he found in urbane society on the two sides of the Atlantic, became at times so overweighted that it almost could not move forward at all.

If Dewey's provinciality left him enabled and emboldened to propose comparatively simple answers to great questions, it helped impose some of his limitations, too. In his pursuit of a model for all human behavior, he was oddly blind to behavior that was not earnest, methodical, and goal-oriented. There are obvious reasons within the logic of his endeavor for this focus on normal behavior, of course, but that does not account for the relentless plainness he projected onto mankind in these early years. One of his coworkers in instrumentalism once referred to Dewey's favorite model for human learning as "that somewhat ponderously curious child with the candle who seems to be taken out of a Dutch interior."[43] When young Dewey sets out to talk about the world as a thing to be studied and explained, it seems to be a world without ecstasy, lacking the incongruous and perverse; it is difficult to think that Dewey's early writings had for their contemporaries A Rebours and The Yellow Book. In a few years Thorstein Veblen would note that Dewey in this period made no allowance for idle curiosity; and others would complain that, for all his remarkable instincts as an educator of the young, he had little sense of the purely pointless play of children. These characteristics of his relate, of course, to the evangelicalism Dewey was raised in, but they also relate, if in a subtler way, to a provincial isolation that marked much of American intellectual life until the 1890s. This isolation was a theme also in the story of the man who would be Dewey's greatest colleague in his philosophy, George Herbert Mead.

George Herbert Mead

In 1902 the Castle family of Hawaii, one of the islands' great sugarcane growers, had printed a memorial edition of the letters of Henry Northrup Castle, a son of the family, who had been drowned in 1895 at the age of thirty-two in a shipwreck on the North Sea. The family had asked Henry's old friend, George Herbert Mead of the University of Chicago's Department of Philosophy, to write a recollection of him for the volume, and Mead's half-dozen pages of reminiscences formed the afterword of the book. [1] What Mead wrote was surprisingly frank for a eulogy. Its theme, quite explicitly, was the protracted, painful search by a talented and idealistic young man for a "stimulus to conduct," a "calling in which he could be himself, and secure the moral action which his nature demanded." Henry's search in the twelve years after he graduated from college had taken him into and out of a newspaper editorship, the law, and professional philosophy. At the end of his sketch, with careful ambiguity, Mead concluded that Castle had at last found "the practical solution" in again turning to the editing of the *Hawaii Gazette*—"an ultimate solution for himself reached only just before his death." Mead, however, had seen Castle's last letters and their cry, "I wish I could *pray*. I wish I could *do*," and he knew that Castle had never found what he was after, that at best he had found only a "practical" solution—one which his death made "ultimate" for him. [2]

Henry Castle's long affliction by "the inability to act when his passionate nature called for expression" will be familiar to those who know Jane Addams's story, in *Twenty Years at Hull House*, of her search for a "field for action." The parallel with Miss Addams goes further, for both Henry Castle and his friend George Herbert Mead also had intensely religious natures and evangelical aspirations. Like her they found they could not in honesty embrace an orthodox religious vocation,, and, again like her, their subsequent search for a secular outlet for their evangelism led them into extended career crises. Henry Castle never found his way, but Mead eventually did. The correspondence Mead carried on with Henry and the Castle family in the years after he and Castle graduated from Oberlin in 1883 tells the story of the two young men. It also helps fix the meaning of the pragmatism of the Chicago School for the men who formulated it.

∞

Mead and Castle first met in 1877 or 1878 when they were both students at the prep school attached to Oberlin College. Mead's father (who was to die in 1878) was an ordained minister and a professor at the college. Henry was the oldest son of Samuel Castle, who as a young man in the years before the Civil War had gone to Hawaii to administer the financial affairs of the Calvinist missions there. By the time Henry was sent back to be educated at Oberlin, his father had become a planter and had begun to amass what would eventually become one of the great fortunes of Hawaii.

It was not until four years after they first met that Mead and Castle became close friends. By then, their junior and senior years, they were two of a type, that minority at any fossilizing denominational college who take the beliefs taught there seriously enough to consider committing their lives to them and reflectively enough to question them. Mead certainly, and perhaps Castle, had been planning to enter the ministry. But the worm of religious doubt had got in, and the two of them had begun to question the Scotch common-sense intuitionalism that was used for defending orthodoxy in the Oberlin classrooms—"A philosophy," Mead called it, "which starts out with the positive doctrine that there must be a consistent philosophy, and finding the only means to it argues that this means must be correct." [3] Mead and Henry Castle took to challenging this orthodoxy in the classroom, and, as editors of the school magazine, they gave Oberlin a taste of literary radicalism. They were "terribly uncompromising" and "in trouble of some kind all the time." By the time they graduated in the summer of 1883 the two friends were agnostics.

Mead, particularly, whether he knew it or not, had been preparing a very bad time for himself. Whatever element of glee had been interlarded with anxiety in his repeated challenges to his teachers now faded away very quickly. Although he had become a skeptic philosophically, his personality and the whole basic set of his aspirations remained exactly what they were a few years earlier, when he had been planning to follow his late father into the ministry. Now, at a loss, he engaged to teach a high school for boys at nearby Berlin Heights. His momentary exultation at being out of college, his resolution not to "pay any attention to my beliefs the moral law or anything of the kind just give myself to a healthy life," faded, and he began to slip into a deep depression. [4] All that fall and winter and into the following spring his letters to Castle (now home in Hawaii, working in his brother's law office) were long, nagging challenges to the orthodox assumption that we can perceive the essences of things and woeful tributes to the strength of Kant's countering arguments that the forms of space and time are strictly subjective. Kant, wrote Mead, "necessitates abandoning the doctrine of immediate perceptions of things in themselves. . . . [T]he externality of space is the keystone to the arch of modern orthodox philosophy and the Samson (to mix the figure) who pulls down this pillar pulls down all modern orthodoxy upon his head." [5] Mead perseverated in letter after letter on Kant's destructive genius, concurred in the denials of the freedom of the will that Castle was in turn writing to him, and became more intensely unhappy by the week. "[M]y sensibilities   seem to be clamoring for Christianity." [6]

> If only I could get a [phrase illegible: "hold on"?] some
> settled beliefs I could find more pleasure in the ministry than
> anywhere in the world. . . . If only I could believe it I could
> find more comfort and infinite relief in the bible in the Peace
> that passeth all understanding than I could begin to find any-
> where else under the sun. [7]

By midwinter he felt he was disintegrating as a person, and in a literal sense he was. In the years of his innocence Mead had been in the blessed state where, to use his own language, "the ideal and action" had been one: God had put us on earth to serve Him and

save one another; the Christian life and the ministry would be at
once fulfillment of this divine plan and self-fulfillment. This
perfect world had now been shattered; agnosticism had introduced Mead to a bleak and tragic notion of existence, and the
shock unhorsed him. He found that he simply could not function
in a world without meaning. His letters showed him com-
pensating for his unbelief by a studied devotion to good works
(and a moralizing, rather ugly impatience with the iniquities of
his fellow man). He tried everything to put his world back
together again: "I have commenced praying and taking part in
religious work. Because I felt the necessity of help out of myself,"
he wrote Henry, early in March of that first year out of college,

> I could not continue any longer with such a flagrant distance
> between the ideal and action and so I tried and succeeded in
> getting help outside of myself. Of course I have not changed
> very materially my views. Except that I believe it is philo-
> sophical to pray. I do not know that there is any God. But in
> some way I get help. It may not reach beyond my own sensi-
> bility but still it gives me help and I need it so much that I can-
> not afford to drop it. If you admit the desirability of such
> harmony between ideal and action such a method of attaining
> [it] becomes perfectly reasonable. Indeed any method which
> did attain it would be reasonable. . . . We both feel that the
> only nobility is in working for others or perhaps for a God if
> there is one, and to refuse to do so is suicidal. [8]

As Mead himself seems to have realized a few months later, he
had come close to a nervous breakdown that winter. At the
height of his misery the town decided to close his school because
of a steadily shrinking enrollment. Mead was crushed and
thought himself a failure, but it was a blessing in disguise. Within
a month he got a job surveying on the railroad outside Saint Paul,
Minnesota. This was physically demanding work; it did not entail
the mental or moral strains that schoolteaching had, and it gave
Mead a chance to stabilize, if not to become any less stricken.
Indeed, his letters of the next three years, during which he
worked with the railroad and then turned to schoolteaching and
tutoring again, seem to lay out a balanced equation of unhappiness. He felt trapped on several scores: on the one hand, he had to
keep working in these uncongenial jobs because his widowed
mother could not underwrite any further education for him and

might need to be supported herself; on the other hand, even should his financial situation ease, he could project no viable future for himself. [9]

Though in that desperate first year he considered hiding his agnosticism and going into the ministry, he seems to have seen that it would be an impossible position to put himself in. The alternative he considered was "metaphysics"; this, he apparently felt, was the one other career that would let him formally, professionally, address the only questions he cared about or that were worth answering. But he couldn't plan on this either. As Henry Castle complained,

> they have no use for philosophers in America. They are utterly superfluous, as a matter of course, in a country where they get their metaphysics by revelation from heaven, and let nobody teach anything in any of the schools and colleges which has not the mark *inspired* on it. [10]

Besides this strictly objective problem of orthodoxy's stranglehold on the philosophy taught in all but a few universities (notably Harvard and Johns Hopkins), Mead was inhibited from planning on a career in philosophy by his own premises about what it was to be a philosopher. In November of 1885 Henry left Hawaii to go to Germany to study philosophy, and several months later the chair in that subject at the University of Minnesota fell vacant. George excitedly wrote his friend that the president of the university was so liberal on religious matters that Henry might be a serious candidate for it. The only impediment in Henry that Mead could anticipate was that he had not yet a system of philosophy of his own devising to promulgate, that he had only a battery of criticisms of the orthodox system of the Scotch intuitionalists. Despite this handicap, Mead advised, Henry could buy time and, meanwhile, "do all you could to stimulate independent thought and lecture upon it. Of course it would be vastly better to have your own system. But it's not necessary from the most conscientious standpoint. Still I doubt not you will have a system long before the year's end." [11] Plainly, Mead was laboring under a very special notion of what it is to be a philosopher. Merely to become a critic of thought or to address oneself to limited questions or areas was not enough. Like the men who had taught him at Oberlin, a philosopher was someone who espoused a system of reality. If one found one could refute the received systems, it was not enough, like Hume, to stand to the side, throw stones at the edifice, and retreat to billiards and obliviousness; if you had destroyed the existing systems, you had to become an Aristotle or a Leibniz and build one in their place.

The grounds of Mead's religious agnosticism, then—his morose conviction that the will is not free and that, with Kant, we are completely trapped in our subjectivity, forever cut off from knowing the world as it is—left him, to his own mind, doubly disabled. Kant, he wrote, "shuts me upon myself and gives me no opportunity of getting out."[12] He had great difficulty in justifying a career of teaching mere criticisms; without a positive philosophy he "would not benefit mankind," and, evangelical that he was, he could see nothing else worth doing. As he wrote Henry, "I cannot literally find a motive sufficient to inspire activity." "[I am left to] play in the twilight with Kant." [13]

It is remarkable how persistently this need for a system dogged Castle and Mead. Mead in one of his long wrestlings cried out, "I want to know what your positive philosophy is, Henry. You must not keep it from me";[14] and several years later, when such an *ignis fatuus* appeared momentarily in front of Henry, he announced triumphantly, "My thought seems to have passed through its critical and negative period, and reached its dogmatic and constructive one."[15] What hope and plans Mead held out for himself in those four years from 1883 to 1887 revolved around the chance of healing his life either through a reacceptance of Christianity and a career in the ministry—a fading possibility— or through escape from surveying and schoolteaching in the provinces to advanced study in the German universities, where he might hope to find at least a secular metaphysic to put order and purpose back into his universe. However, his feeling of responsibility for his mother's financial well-being hung heavy on him, and he couldn't get away. The frustration of his young ambitions and energies told on him. He haunted himself with self-doubting: "I am not you know a powerful person. I have not much creative energy. ... I am lacking in aggressive force." [16] Predictably, he openly envied the "naturals" among their old Oberlin classmates, those uncomplicated souls who were simply making their way in the world. Of one: "He smokes, drinks and sees hardly any harm in patronizing houses of ill-repute," but, "he has more power than me and my nature rebels against it. . . . This worldly success hangs over me like a nightmare and has a power which dashes all my philosophy and appreciation my moral sense and ideal into pitiable insignificance. What are they worth!"[17] Groan under it as he might, Mead's inability to go the way of the world—his refusal to go into the law, for instance ("I am afraid that [I] should degenerate into a mere money getting animal")[18]—held the seed of his future identity and greatness; it kept him searching for a philosophy that would make meaning and ideals out of human experience—a substitute for the Christianity of his childhood. In the meantime he was drawing no comfort from a future he didn't know: "How one longs for fiery action that could swallow up all this inaction and imbecile cowardice."[19] "My life looks dreary and fruitless. . . . This is a sapless dying tree," he wrote Henry early in 1885, and within a month he developed a kidney disease which, he confided to his friend, would probably kill him. The doctor, it goes without saying, could find no sign of it.[20]

In the fall of 1886 Henry Castle turned from German philosophy to go to Harvard to study law. He exercised his option to take courses in other areas of the university by attending classes in the Department of Philosophy, particularly those of Josiah Royce. That same year there occurred a subtle but definite change in Mead's mood and thinking about his own future. His mother was now happily teaching at Oberlin and hoped to continue doing it for another five or six years. Thanks to this unburdening, and encouraged perhaps by the example of Henry at Harvard, there began to push through the mould of Mead's continuing religious crisis some definite hopes and plans for himself. In October he wrote Henry that he was "going to cut loose" the next year for four years of study of philosophy at Berlin or some comparable university; first, though, he would "try . . . for a fellowship at Johns Hopkins." In midwinter he fell sick and again faded off into despondency; but in April, in a letter in which he complained again about his want of "a motive sufficient to inspire activity" and about the wearisomeness of his investigation of Christianity, he was begging Henry for advice on getting scholarships, and two weeks later—though ill again—he was by his own description "ready to try anything anywhere." Not even the drudgeries of everyday life could "extinguish the hope and

expectation that under the appropriate circumstances I could
blossom out . . . O for an opportunity."

> I can begin to see more pleasure in life than I have this winter.
> A great many things begin to assume worthy colors and attract
> me again. Especially would life seem desirable if I could find
> my life opening out upon some fine object upon which I could
> become really enthusiastic. Such a purpose is the one essen-
> tial. . . . There must be room for action for us. . . . I will get
> to work and find what life has for me. [21]

That summer Mead's ambitions for himself and for a meaning-
ful life finally fashioned the "opportunity" he had been looking
for. By borrowing and by committing himself to tutor while
studying there, he managed, barely managed—it was August
before he could be sure—to scrape together enough money to get
to Harvard for the coming school year. Henry, who that spring
had briefly considered leaving Harvard Law and returning to
Germany and philosophy, cheered him on, his great inducement
a promise that Mead would be able to take a course with him and
one other student under Royce—"*Reading Kant.*" [22]

It is a measure of Josiah Royce's impact that he could make
Castle exclaim with joy at the prospect of studying Kant with
him. Kant, after all, had figured in Castle's life and in Mead's as a
skeptic and a destroyer. But Henry's excitement was not
misplaced, for the Kant they were to hear about in Royce's
classrooms was a philosopher who not only introduced man to
doubt and subjectivism but also showed him where he might find
the courage to live with it—a Kant, as Royce put it,

> whom a long experience of problems makes skeptical above all
> men, cautious, critical, resigned to doubts, a hater of mystical
> faith, a destroyer of dogmas; and yet he gives us back our
> faith, not as a dogma, but as an active postulate, as a free
> spiritual construction, as a determination to live in the
> presence of the unseen and eternal. [23]

Mead, speaking thirty years later about the book in which
Royce popularized the points of view he had been teaching his
students when Mead was among them, suggested that there
should be "a special edition of the *Spirit of Modern Philosophy*
bound in tooled morocco with illuminated borders and initialed
paragraphs and illustrated with pre-Raphaelite art—to symbolize

what it meant to young men when Royce first taught in Cambridge."[24] It is uncanny the way passages in the *Spirit of Modern Philosophy* seem to speak to Mead and Castle; a good example is Royce's peculiar dramatization of the message in Kant's *Critique of Practical Reason*:

> Evil besets us, pain oppresses us, chagrin or calamity over-
> whelms us. We cry out bitterly, "Prove to me that such a life
> is good. Experience doesn't show it to be good. And as for
> faith, as for intuitive trust that it is good, this I have lost.
> My noble sentiments fade out; my natural love of life forsakes
> me. Is it all tolerable? Prove that to me."
> The answer of the active temperament, the answer which
> seems so stern to us in our moments of weakness and
> cowardice, so inspiring to us in our moments of spiritual
> dignity and courage, is the answer: "Your world is tolerable,
> yes, is even glorious, if, and only if, you actively make it so.
> Its spirituality is your own creation, or else is nothing. Awake,
> arise, be willing, endure, struggle, defy evil, cleave to good,
> strive, be strenuous, be devoted, throw into the face of evil
> and depression your brave cry of hatred and of resistance, and
> then this dark universe of destiny will glow with a divine
> light." [25]

We have no way of knowing what, precisely, Mead took from Royce; he and his friend Henry lived together in a lodging at 11 Sumner Street in Cambridge, and so they had no need to exchange letters. As it turned out, Mead had been too tired the summer before he went to Harvard to master German well enough to take the seminar in Kant. However, he did audit Royce's courses, and in his memorial he credited Royce with showing him "a vision that followed me for many years." The vision as he described it was the intellectual style of Royce's speculative idealism:

> What had been barriers of thought became but hazards in the
> game. Contradictions [such as Kant's criticisms of the
> common-sense notions of time and space, which had frozen
> Mead into a dumb and horrified agnosticism], instead of
> marking the no thoroughfares of reflection, became the guide
> posts toward higher levels of reality. . . . [There was] an
> impression . . . of freedom of mind, and of dominance of
> thought in the universe, of a clear unclouded landscape of

spiritual reality where we sat like gods together—but not
careless of mankind. [26]

The emphasis is not on the specific content of Royce's absolute
idealism (it seems likely that Mead did not become a thorough
convert to it) but on a posture, a membership in a brotherhood of
young men who had experienced the death of old faiths and were
now making liberal or even secular vessels for their idealism.

While Mead was being funded by Royce and by such authors
as T. H. Green, whom he also read that first year at Harvard,
with the resources that could put him at peace with his
agnosticism, he was also being swept up in the round of graduate
life at Harvard—in ambitions and hard work and some excitement and gratification. It was good for him, and his petty
moralism disappeared, along with the vague metaphysical
longings and general neuroticism (Royce referred to the nineteenth century as "the century of nerves and spiritual sorrows")
that had plagued him over the preceding five years. In the fall
term he took G. H. Palmer's course in ethics, Spinoza and
Spencer with Royce, two Greek courses, a course in philosophy
with Francis Bowen (then clearly a holdover from the old days
before Harvard had been infected with the modern university
spirit—"old Bowen," Castle called him in a letter home), [27] and
sat in on the Kant seminar. In the spring he took a similar
program.

Henry, meanwhile, was following the regular law-school
curriculum and, of course, Royce. In March, however, in one of
those fits of disappointment with himself that characterized him
all his life, Henry decided that he would only be evading reality
by further study and that he ought to go home to Hawaii and his
family responsibilities. He was there in the early summer to
receive two letters from Mead, summing up his year. The first
one was a mixture of closely calculated anticipation and of
triumph: Mead was on the edge of receiving high grades in
several courses but might miss them all; however, his honors
exam in philosophy had gone very well:

Palmer complimented me upon my appearance and William
James the next morning came round to look me up and told me
he wants me to go out with him this summer and teach his
boy . . .; Prof. James told me that he had several applications
for the place but that I took care of myself so well in the

examination that he wished me especially as he could then have someone to whom he could talk metaphysics. [28]

Mead's second letter announced jubilantly that he had taken his degree *magna cum laude*. "I am now going to have a Ph.D. from Berlin at any cost," he wrote, and his plans for financing this revealed a well-developed feel for the politics of graduate aid. [29]

Some weeks later Mead wrote Henry from James's summer place that his host and employer had received a letter from George Santiana [*sic*] indicating that he might come back from Germany and "develop out of his disgust a system if he has sufficient audacity to." Santayana had hopes of being allowed to keep his Harvard traveling fellowship despite his return to Cambridge, but it was Mead's guess that this wouldn't be allowed and that the fellowship would fall open. "I should apply for it and there is a dim possibility that I should get it. But the competition is so strong." [30] Whether it was on this or another scholarship, that autumn found Mead in Leipzig studying philosophy and physiological psychology.

Some years later, in 1891 and 1892, physiological psychology was to take on a wholly extraordinary meaning in Mead's life and thought, but the auspices under which he entered into the study of it now, in 1888, were ordinary — typical of the times and of the more or less matter-of-fact career-building into which Mead was redirecting his energies. Even before his year at Harvard and his contact with William James, Mead indicated in a letter to Henry that he understood the use being made of the new psychology in contemporary philosophical thought:

> What a contrast there is between the mental philosophers of 100 years ago and the busy student of idiots and the insane the hunter after nerves and nerve ganglions the discusser of methods of pedagogics. . . . [T]he scientific spirit of modern psychology . . . saves the class of philosophers as a whole from wasting themselves upon to them meaningless formulae. [31]

Why, in brief, continue to base assertions about the nature of the mind on introspection and deduction when all the physical accompaniments of cerebration might now be measured exactly in a laboratory? [32] Its promise along these lines and James's interest in it may have attracted Mead to it; but as much or more to the point, as far as he was concerned, was the chance for a career that it offered. It was still a very new and underpopulated area in American departments of philosophy, and it might be a particularly useful attainment in view of the fact that most academic positions were still in denominational colleges. Given his unorthodoxy, Mead assumed he would have trouble; "it would be hard for him," Henry wrote to his parents in Hawaii, "to get a chance to utter any ultimate philosophical opinions savoring of independence. In Physiological Psychology on the other hand he has a harmless territory in which he can work quietly without drawing down upon himself the anathema and excommunication of all-potent Evangelicism." [33]

Mead had been in Leipzig only a month or two when he was joined by Castle. Once again Henry had found himself restless and unfulfilled in Hawaii and had come early that fall to visit Harvard and then Columbia with an eye to completing his law degree; he had decided against it in each place and was now intending to study a mix of law, philosophy, and political economy at a German university with George. In February the two students moved on to the University of Berlin. Mead was to stay there for almost three years, until October or November of 1891, working toward his doctorate. Castle stayed with Mead for the first of those three academic years, went back to Hawaii the second year with his German bride, and upon her tragic accidental death returned to Berlin for the third year.

What they saw and read in Germany had a deep effect on the young friends. Like their experiences with Royce and Harvard, it introduced them to perspectives on human affairs that were undreamed of at a place like Oberlin. Except for an extraordinary group of letters which he wrote to Henry when his wife died, there survive almost no communications from Mead for these three years (the two friends lived together the first and third years and, as we shall see, Mead let their correspondence lapse almost completely during the year of Henry's marriage). Consequently, Henry's letters to his family are our principal source for this period. What emerges from them is a picture that had hundreds of duplicates: young Americans being captivated by the atmosphere and goings-on in the German universities, by the air of discovery and of political importance that surrounded especially the burgeoning social sciences. Mead's and Castle's susceptibility had already been prepared by their rasping, fruitless struggles with the abstract, interior, and private issues of Oberlin

religion and by their encounter with Josiah Royce. Royce had
primed them by teaching them that the only compensation for
their loss of childhood faith was to be found in "the acceptance by
the individual of the common life and common interest as his
own, ... the substitution of the social and universal for the
private and particular." It is "the common organic life of
mankind which is the ethical ideal," and it is "only because we
cannot surrender the selfish dream of a private happiness, that
we still long for any other immortality."[34] This was brave and
moving stuff that Henry would write to his parents but, as he
himself sensed, it was frightfully vague; it "leaves the question,
still open, of what is this social life to consist, what are its
activities." Once in Germany Henry began immediately to see a
content for his ethical ideal. In March 1889, not five months after
he had arrived in Leipzig, he was telling his sister:

> I have awaked in the last two years to a whole class of facts,
> to a side of life of which I was unconscious before, or rather to
> which my eyes were closed, and that is to all phases of
> contemporary social and political development. ... I have
> waked from my individualistic dream. ... I am as much
> interested in speculation as ever but most intensely interested
> in the practical applications.[35]

So Henry took courses in ethics and philosophy, but he also began
to push himself through Wilhelm Wundt's *Physiological Psychology*, the epitome of *Wissenschaft* ("diabolic," Henry found it,
but, "I wade along"),[36] and he turned to political economy. "The
social question—the labor question—is the most pressing problem
and the most imminent danger of our times," he intoned to his
parents,

> and to deal with it, to ameliorate social conditions, to elevate
> the working class and moderate the extremes of social
> inequality is the essential task of civilization in this century.
> The only preparation for dealing with it successfully is in the
> careful study of anthropology and sociology, of Political
> Economy and Economic history. In addition to these must
> come experience and practical sense. Social reform schemes
> which will not work may as well be laid on the shelf.[37]

And so Henry found himself for once "working steadily, and

happily, along." But he had fallen in love with their German
landlady's very lovely nineteen-year-old daughter, and once
again (inevitably, it would seem) he got sidetracked: they decided
to wed that fall. He went to the great Friedrich Paulsen, whose
Ethics he had found so inspiring, and asked him to direct his
doctoral thesis. The topic Henry proposed was in keeping with his
now exultant vision of the possibilities of life. He would write his
thesis "on the relation of Christianity to a reasoned system of
ethics or to the modern scientific view of life in general." Paulsen
was not swept away by Henry's plan to redeem Christianity: "He
told me the object of a thesis is not to show capacity for
independent thought, but for *gelehrsame Arbeit*, and accordingly
the proper thing for me to do is to hunt up some musty and
neglected corner of the history of philosophy, and spend a year
studying it."[38] Frustrated by this ugly fact of life and finding
himself quite lost by the lectures in German political economy he
was attending at the university, Henry decided to return to
America, to either Harvard or Columbia, where he could finish
up his law degree while continuing to study political economy.
He thought that he had only a year's work to do to gain the
degree in law; but when he got to Cambridge, Harvard
demanded longer residence of him. He couldn't countenance the
delay, so he and Frida, his bride, continued on to Hawaii in
November.

What we can learn of George Mead's interior life during these
two years—the first with Henry in Leipzig and Berlin, the
second, after Henry's marriage, when he lived alone in Berlin—
we find out only indirectly through Henry's references to his
friend in his own correspondence (we have already seen his
account of George's reasons for concentrating on physiological
psychology). In a letter written at the height of his political
enthusiasms in March 1889, Henry confided to his brother that he
and his roommate George had agreed on a plan whereby Henry
would finish his German Ph.D. and go to practice law in
Honolulu for a few years, while George would finish his and teach
in an American university: "The idea is that after a half-dozen
years in Honolulu, I will have a little money, and he will have
reputation. Then we think we may pool the two and start our
paper."[39] This "paper" was to be a reforming city newspaper.
Evidently, then, George was also fascinated by "the social ideal,"
and he collaborated with Henry's effort to sort out the roles men

might play in the great reform movement. "About *Looking Backward* I have come round to your way of thinking in the essential points," Henry wrote to George on one occasion in 1889. "The place to air Socialism is from the Chair of a Sociological or Ethical Professor. A newspaper man* should confine himself to practical ends and measures."[40]

The very fragmentary evidence indicates that this was not an easy year for Mead personally. That summer, as Henry was preparing to get married, George received a scolding letter from William James. Whatever was behind it, James apparently accused Mead of having on some particular occasion made an ass of himself; Mead was mightily stung by the phrase, and he and James had no more concourse with each other until a year and a half later, when James sent his *Psychology* to Mead as it came off the press. After Henry and his bride left Europe, Mead continued on at Berlin and became engaged to an American girl there. In November or December he wrote Henry two letters, one telling the news and the other, shortly afterward, telling of a rather bad physical accident he had had and of his fears (apparently never borne out) that it would leave him with a disability.[41] This was the last letter he wrote Henry for almost nine months. Then one day, shortly after he had sadly seen the end of his engagement, word reached him of the death of Henry's wife.

∽

MY DEAR GEORGE—
    I have not heard from you since last December—and presume this note will never reach you but send it on the chance. How are you—and what are you doing—let me know. Please write me. I have been in the depths. . . .

Mead sensed that his old friend was pleading with him for a context in which he might come to terms with the loss of his wife, and in the long letters Mead wrote Henry in the ensuing weeks he

---

*Edward Bellamy, who wrote *Looking Backward*, was editor of a newspaper in Springfield, Massachusetts. Henry's letter continued: "*Looking Backward* simply turns a lot of simple heads topsy turvy. Still it rouses the attention of better minds."

responded with an intimate account of the world he saw. It was a stark vision:

> For two years the grandeur of the heavens has given way with me before the arbitrariness of this side of the universe. . . . I have found nothing but meaninglessness in these balls whirling about with various forms of conscious life eking out a dubious existence on the thin decaying surfaces.

> The thought of the heavens has become almost intolerable because of the sameness and lack of reason or meaning . . . and the effort to find the meaning along these lines of the physical sciences and the elementary axiomatic and hence utterly arbitrary laws of dynamics comes in the same despairing time with the opening of one's eyes to the limits of the expectations of early years. Why shouldn't one strive to give a boy a modest practical conception of the world he is coming into, save novels and poetry till they should feed a healthy aesthetic sense instead of painting a world that doesn't exist . . . and with whose vanishing much of the ideal [side of life] must be carried off too? [42]

Mead went on to give a specific etiology for what he called "this sense of double disappointment in life and thought." It had to do with a conviction that had descended on him that, as he put it, "the spacial side was as really one side [of the universe] as the thought side."[43] He was experiencing the realization that overcame so many Victorians when they encountered modern physics and evolutionary science, a sudden awareness of "the accidental character of mankind on earth," in Mead's words. One thinks of Henry Adams at the death of his sister, watching the apparent loveliness of Mont Blanc stripped away to reveal the mountain's true nature—a chaos of elemental forces. In Mead's case, of course, it was also a rephrasing of his earlier crisis: once again, the universe was indifferent to man; he was alone with his needs. If we are to credit his dating of it ("two years"), it would appear that Mead fell into this mood when he first came to Germany in the late summer of 1888, after leaving the world of William James and, most especially, of Josiah Royce (whose philosophical idealism, after all, it must have been that had left Mead hoping that the "thought side" of the universe might be more real than "the spacial side"). Along with his medical difficulties, the troubled romance, and so forth, this renewed anticipation "of the shipwreck of our individual ends and values"[44] and of the arbitrariness of the cosmos had darkened his two years. But now, he confided to Henry, he had found a way out by an "almost despairing effort to push away from our standpoint here and force a combination in which the accidental and yet the constructive can be combined." Like all of Mead's crises and solutions, it was at once intimately personal and abstract to the last degree:

> The greatest conquest I have made in these last days is the confident belief that space is a construction of our eye—that the three dimensions rest simply upon the optic nerve and the sense of touch and especially the hand. The system of the Heavens, the innumerable balls swinging in space which seem so meaningless as even one side of the universe rest for their form upon the most artificial and complicated of instruments, the eye and the hand. [45]

Space itself, then, the vastness of the universe, which had been so oppressive to Mead, was only a construction of our organs of sense. Robbed of its absoluteness, it became less frightening. But what then? Space gone, where are we?

> We must decentralize the eyes as well as the earth. So much must remain that we are in our actual position only very insignificant most intricately constructed forms to be sure, that rise to selfconsciousness, but occupying a side position, an unimportant position in the history of the whole. However we may construct the forms in which we cast our sensations we do not construct the history that takes its shape in them, and our position in that history in comparison with the whole is still the true position, and finding that position out of any direct line with the whole so that our line of vision does not fall in with the great line of advance—that we look at things from the side and always reconstruct we can understand that the view we get from the standpoint of our organs . . . must be as imperfect as a man taken alone and considered the result and worthy sum total of all is imperfect.

The letter went on and on, the punctuation scarcer and scarcer, as Mead tried to explain to Henry what he saw. It was a most chastened evolutionary prospect, but it turned out that he *was* offering hope and therapy to his bereaved friend, the therapy that so many people in that generation eventually came to: selfabnegation, and a casting of their personal lot with the lot of mankind in an ideal of service. In another letter of this period,

Mead wrote: "Only in one direction is it satisfactory—the historical—the process—the method—the laws—the constant advance."[46] Invoking the models of German social and municipal reform and of the English philosophical radical and Liberal Party statesman, John Morley, Mead urged Henry to return to Germany:

> ... the immediate necessity is that we should have a clear conception of what forms socialism is taking in [the] life of European lands especially of the organisms of municipal life—how cities sweep their streets, manage their gas works and street cars—their Turnvereins, their houses of prostitution, their poor their minor criminals their police etc. etc., that one may come with ideas to the American work.
>
> Now Henry you must come and at least get such a share in these subjects and hold of the social political literature that you can go right on when we are back. I must teach at first for I must earn money but I shan't keep at it long. I want more active life and I feel that this phys. psy. [physiological psychology] gives me exactly the right sort of foundation for this work. My vague plan now is that I go to the University of Minnesota as a teacher—and you to Minneapolis as a lawyer and that we finally get control of the Minneapolis Tribune. This is of course hazy. ...
>
> The world is a lonely place, I know that we are walking along the bank of the largest and deepest stream of life and satisfactory life—that in nature and society God expresses himself if he could only be read but it doesn't belong to our day to read him and every time I attempt to make the spring into the current I feel as if I tried to step into the fourth dimension of space. We have to deny ourselves great emotions and great upliftings, but not the satisfactoriness of thinking and acting that is above the pettiness and low desires and filth of narrow egotisms. I have a growing faith that we can live calmly and greatly ... if not gloriously and deeply.

"If not gloriously and deeply." It is remarkable, really, how the letters that Mead poured out in these late summer days of 1890 summed up and brought to a temporary resolution the themes of the previous decade in his life. In the interests of ascertaining exactly what it was that his coming contact with John Dewey and his entry into Dewey's philosophy would do for him, it may be worth our time to make certain aspects of his experience and reflections even more explicit. We have seen that, beginning sometime late in his college days, Mead had hungered after a restoration of the wholeness he had lost when he lost his faith at Oberlin. He wanted a world that made sense and answered man's spiritual needs—a world he could work *for* through a vocation, through the ministry or some analogue of it that would give him "a motive sufficient to inspire activity." It has often been said of the American Progressives of his generation (especially of Dewey) that they were looking to restore a vision of their childhoods, trying to lure industrial America back to the orderly rural towns they had grown up in. In Mead's case, certainly, this is inaccurate, though he *was* searching for something lost. His letters to Henry Castle in August and September of 1890 make it clear that he had not found it but that he was reaching a sort of accommodation. The cosmos was, as likely as not, utterly devoid of meaning, but this was a call to a dis-illusioned heroism. He wrote to Henry that they must "get together and deliberately set about some social and political work":

> I don't mean [as] an ideal but as [a] line of activity. I am perfectly willing to fail. Life looks like such an insignificant affair that two or three or more years of utterly unsuccessful work would not seem to me in the slightest dampening, and the subjective satisfaction of actually doing what my nature asked for of infinitely more importance than anything else. [47]

First he must finish his degree and teach for a year or two to pay off his debts. As for the role of physiological psychologist itself, his letters make it clear that it would be only a means to an end; he could commit himself to it only to the degree that it yielded useful tools, "the psychology of early moral development," for instance. [48] It was not of itself the vocation that his evangelical soul still wanted.

In November of that year, 1890, Henry responded to George's urgings and left Hawaii for Germany. There he joined his sister Helen, who had been in Europe when Henry's wife had been killed and who was already at George's side. "I need not tell you," Henry wrote his parents, "what a rock and stronghold for us two nervous shattered people George Mead is." [49] In his dreamy, uncertain way Henry readdressed himself to philosophy and political economy. As George had predicted, it proved therapeutic. So also, apparently, did the work of translating short German works on educational psychology to which Mead had set Helen. Mead himself pressed on toward his doctorate. Sometime that winter he and Helen became engaged, and his need to finish and to get a university position in the United States became more acute (and thoughts of the newspaper—which figured in his correspondence until as late as November—more remote). Though he had not considered it likely that he would be offered a position before he returned to America, the University of Michigan in late May or early June (1891) offered Mead an instructorship in the Department of Philosophy. "I regard it as a brilliant opening," Henry wrote to his parents; "Ann Arbor presents a promising field of influence. Thought is measurably free there, not harnessed to the Juggernaut of any church *ism*. He would be a co-worker with Professor Dewey, one of America's leading men."[50] The formal offer from the trustees was followed by "a delightful letter from Prof. Dewey"; and some weeks later, while he and Helen, now married, were in the Harz Mountains, Mead received from Dewey an outline of his academic duties for the following year. He recounted them to Henry:

> The Phys. Psy. I have to myself—a course in the History of Phil—and a half course in Kant—and another on Evolution. Doesn't it make your mouth water, my boy—come and do likewise eventually. My head is full of schemes for the course—especially for the Hist. of Phil. . . . Kant will be a most admirable dessert. The drudgery will be the Phys. Psy. for I shan't have much opportunity for original work and to use it for pedagogical purposes is hard.[51]

Mead apparently received permission to stay on in Germany after the beginning of the fall semester at Michigan in order to complete his residency requirements for the Berlin Ph.D. and also, perhaps, the thesis itself. This latter Mead described as "largely a criticism from a Kantian or at least Metaphysical standpoint of the sensational doctrine of space—and finally a reconstruction of the facts from a speculative standpoint."[52] It appears from this that Mead was using his dissertation to develop the insight he had excitedly communicated to Henry a year earlier when he "awoke" to the realization that space "is only the construction of our organs of sense" and thus simply an element in the economy of human perception to be studied and understood by philosophical epistemology, that is, "from a speculative standpoint." Now as then he allowed that he was finding the work of the physiological psychologists a useful ancillary:

> I have acquired a respect for the work done and the men who have done it on the subject which is far beyond what I had three months ago. A steady clearing up of the physical processes, and unflinching determination to express the facts of sensation with perfect simplicity are features [which] call for enthusiasm when one finds them free from all bitterness of polemicism and always kept fresh by constant contact with mother nature. Such men as Hering, Helmholst, Stumpf one must doff his hat to. [53]

Mead was even willing to deem William James's close friend, Carl Stumpf, more than a psychologist—he was a philosopher, a man of "real speculative depth."

Try as he might, it turned out that Mead could not coordinate his official residency at the university and the completion of his thesis in a way that would satisfy the regulations for taking the degree. He pleaded "with great unction with the Dekan and Professors Dilthey and Zeller, but though they were very kind and appreciative and cudgelled their brains for some way out they could find none."[54] Reluctantly, he decided he would have to return to Europe the following summer to take his degree. Henry had already left for Hawaii, and in November George and his wife left Berlin for Ann Arbor.

8   The Emergence of Dewey's Pragmatism

Mead was blessed in the moment he happened to come to the University of Michigan's Department of Philosophy. The *Thought News* episode was percolating along toward what would be its climax in the spring of the new year, and Dewey, his chairman, was giving much of his time to it. Dewey's mood of exultation and creativity had another base, besides. It had been five years now since his bold entrance into the philosophical world with the articles in *Mind*, in which he had declared that since, as Hegel had shown, the world is mind and since psychology is the study of mind, psychology rather than metaphysics is the study of the universe, of all reality; psychology *is* philosophic method. That had been in 1886. The reader of those articles could have been pardoned for expecting that Dewey would shortly begin to fulfill the implied promise of his new position, that he would begin to show how psychology—especially "the new psychology," experimental and physiological—gives a more adequate and revealing account of reality than does metaphysics. If psychology is *the* method for philosophy, then let us see it at work. Such an expectation would have been disappointed; certainly, Dewey's *Psychology* textbook did not fill the bill. Dewey wrote another article or two for *Mind* defending the premises of his new standpoint, but they contained no hoped-for revelations, no effulgent new reading of reality. Instead, so far as any audience he had could tell, he had largely turned his attention toward ethics.

Actually, this wasn't so. The ethics itself was being turned more and more into an analysis of behavior, a psychology, and Dewey was keeping his mind very much on that area and on metaphysics. He brought out somewhat revised editions of his *Psychology* in 1889 and 1891, the revisions being in each instance away from philosophical idealism and toward scientific statement of the processes of mind. Still, there was no sign of the advent of a new epoch in our understanding of the world. Then, suddenly it seems, in late 1891, in the midst of his excitement over the *Thought News* revolution, he found what he had been looking for. His first sighting of it was an indistinct one, and he certainly would not have published it. We know about it because it was Dewey's turn to teach the department's introduction to philosophy in the spring term of that school year, and he took this duty as his occasion to draw up a syllabus in which he began to recast philosophy in the light of his new insight. [1]

What he produced was confused and amateurish, full of Fordian enthusiasms. Nevertheless, it indicates what he was trying to do. In March, a month after he had begun to teach the course it outlined, he sent a copy of the first part of the syllabus to James Angell, who had graduated in philosophy from Michigan in June of the previous year and was now doing graduate work with William James at Harvard. "There is no doubt," he wrote Angell,

> of the need of some simpler and more direct attack upon philosophy than any now existing. I have no doubt personally that the main truths of philosophy can be stated in a natural self-commending manner beyond anything now anticipated. When the present ferment shall have subsided and matters are settled down in the intellectual life, I believe it will be found easier to give a man the main standpoint, method, and categories of philosophy than to give him those of a science. . . . I am indeed already trying an experiment in my introduction to phil. I send you pages as far as published. [2]

The syllabus began:

> Philosophy (science) is the conscious inquiry into experience. It is the attempt of experience to attain to its own validity and fullness; the realization of the meaning of experience. . . .
> The only distinction between Science and philosophy is that the latter reports the more generic (wider) features of life; the former the more detailed and specific. [3]

Dewey then made some remarks on the history of thought: science, he implied, had overspecialized and lost sight of the whole it had originally set out to illuminate; philosophy in turn had become vague and "metaphysical"—understandably, for it is only insofar as the "whole is really attained in experience, [that] it becomes possible to treat it in a direct, natural way, *but only in so far."* Now, however, things had begun to come together again:

> In two directions, the whole is now more definitely realized
> than ever before, so that we have a language for reporting it.
> These two directions are the two phases of action. On one
> hand, science has revealed to us, in outline, at least, the type
> action of the individual organism, the process involved in every
> complete act. On the other hand, as life has become freer,
> social action has revealed the principle involved in it. The
> action of the psycho-physical and of the political body, in other
> words, give us such perception of the whole that we may
> report the latter, thus translating philosophical truth into
> common terms.

This second "action," the political, was of course Dewey's
reference to his and Franklin Ford's syndicalism and to *Thought
News*. It is the former action, "the type action of the individual
organism," that is the important one here. "The unit of nervous
action is called the reflex arc," he began.

> This term covers not simply the narrower "reflex" of physiology
> (the winking of an eye, for example) but every unified action,
> or completed portion of conduct. *Illustrations*: the movement
> of an amoeba, the impulse of a child for food, the perception
> of color, a word like "civilization," with its whole meaning, a
> virtuous act, a philosophic theory. Each is a unified action;
> and in this unity of action various conditions are brought to a
> head or focussed. Each is a co-ordination of certain experi-
> ences; each is an *expression*, more or less direct, more or less
> explicit, of the whole of life; it is the manifold circumstance
> of the Universe attaining a unity in action.
>   Such an activity as finds expression then in an entire reflex-
> arc is a whole, a concrete, an individual. It is the *Self* in more
> or less developed form.

What was happening here was that Dewey had groped his way
to the most important step in his movement from Hegelianism to
instrumentalism. Five years earlier he had secured his reduction
of the universe to Mind; now he was reducing, so to speak, the
whole idealist description of Mind to a single model—the
stimulus-response reflex arc of the psychologists. As he said,
whether it was "the impulse of a child for food," or the process of
perception, or concept formation, or the most complex and

extended conceivable human activity, say the formation of "a philosophic theory," each can be described perfectly on the reflex-arc model. It is clear what his purpose was: to be able to say that the universe is entirely expressed in the model, that the reflex arc *is* the universe:

> In the type action, we have the universe expressed, and from its [the "type-action's," the reflex arc's] structure, therefore, we may read the main philosophic ideas. Every such action is representative of the whole because it *is* the whole in con- centrated form, *not* because it is part of the whole.

What follows from this should be obvious: all the experimenta- tion being done in Germany and America and elsewhere on the reflex arc would by this stroke be transformed into a vast scientific inquiry into Mind, into all the classic questions of philosophy, metaphysics, ethics, and so forth. Dewey would have founded philosophy on experimental science.

The syllabus of his course indicates that Dewey spent much of the semester showing how the principal distinctions and cate- gories of philosophy derived from his "type action." Of Will and Intelligence he said, for instance:

> There are . . . two sides in the reflex-arc. These sides have no separation in fact, but may be distinguished by us. One side is the *diversity* of conditions involved; the other side is the *unity of action*.
>   To the unity corresponds the Self as Will; to the diversity, the Self as Intelligence.

Again, within Intelligence and knowledge we have, classically, two sides, the sensory and the ideal. "The multiple conditions involved in an act" constitute the sensory side of knowledge; any one of them "constitutes a sensation or a stimulus." On the other side, the "diverse conditions, or minor acts, involved within a unified action, have also their adjustments to each other. Each holds in check the others, and in turn is held by them. . . . This mutual checking and re-inforcing . . . is the relation of the *sensory* element. *It is thus the ideal side of knowledge.*" Dewey continued on, class after class, showing how categories could be derived from the central model of organic behavior, how particular and universal, cause and effect, mechanical and organic, etc., etc., all represented ways of looking at the act, or moments within it. And, of couse, any act is a reflex arc.

Students of Dewey or people who have read his most important and perhaps most famous essay, "The Reflex Arc Concept in Psychology," published in 1896, should at this point be experiencing some uneasiness with what Dewey was doing in his 1892 *Syllabus of Course 5.*[4] "The Reflex Arc" article of 1896 was, after all, not a celebration of the reflex-arc construct but a criticism of it as an inadequate model of human behavior. Dewey had not come to this conclusion when he put together the syllabus; but a few months later, in April 1892, he had occasion to write another letter to James Angell, and by then he had begun to change his mind. Angell had written to Dewey complaining about the lack of a direction in the field of physiological psychology. "I agree with what you say about phys. psy.," Dewey responded, "*on present methods*, i.e. experimenting without any universal or principle." But, he went on, the philosophy department at Ann Arbor had come up with a "general conception":

It fits in well with the present movement of phil. and psy. thought and I believe will offer a hypothesis for unifying mental phenomena which can be tested in the laboratory. If this is so experiment can be carried on to some purpose. Of course I can't explain the theory here in detail, but it starts with the assumption of the "reflex arc" or circuit as I should call it, a unit of all phenomena, that is

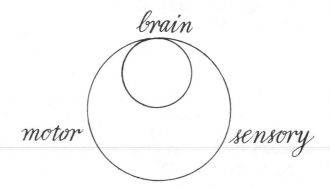

The process *all the way round* is assumed to be the unit—
every such unit is an object or experience, the very motor
outgo (attention) creating what is (psychically) a new object,
through changing the sensory conditions.

Without going into further detail, I think it is obvious that
this affords some meaning for studies of time reactions,
rhythm, time perception and attention. I hope I may get a
chance to talk it all over with you. We are just getting it into
shape for some laboratory experimenting ourselves. [5]

What is most to be noticed here is Dewey's movement away from
the model of the *arc* toward that of the *circuit*. Even in
the syllabus he had composed earlier that year there is evidence
that what he wanted to express was comporting ill with the
stimulus-response arc. Everything in his intellectual background,
from his early admiration of Thomas Huxley's physiology
textbook to Hegelianism, had led him to look for entelechy
and organic growth in his subjects, whereas the reflex arc had an
undeniable jerkiness to it. Stimulus–response, stimulus–idea–
response, stimulus–idea–response . . .: it was too much a series of
discrete happenings with no necessary implication of self-actual-
ization, accumulation, incorporation, growth. Moreover, it was
fundamentally at odds with an epistemological point Dewey had
spent much ink on: that nothing is really external to the mind,
that what we call sensation is a stage *within* the idea ("the
sticking point to a successful statement of idealism," Dewey
called this doctrine). [6] The reflex-arc paradigm suggested, on the
contrary, an event or object in some outside world bursting in on
a torpid consciousness and rousing it to a response. In the syllabus
Dewey had dealt with this by simply insisting, though without
much defense of his position, that sensing is itself an *act* on the
part of the organism. It was tensions such as these between the
reflex-arc theory and Dewey's requirements of a theory of human
conduct that led him over the next several years to work out the
model he finally unveiled in 1896 with the publication of "The
Reflex Arc Concept in Psychology."

The reflex-arc concept is a profoundly misleading representa-
tion of human behavior, this remarkable article began. Take the
commonest illustration of it, the example in which the child is
stimulated by light from a candle into grasping it and is then
stimulated by the burn of the flame into withdrawing his hand.

Stimulus–response, stimulus–response? Not at all. Such a "description" of the little drama is really an interpretation imposed from without, one that falsifies the event. The real beginning here is not a sensation or stimulus; the "real beginning is with the act of seeing; it is looking, and not a sensation of light":

> We begin not with a sensory stimulus, but with a sensori-motor
> coordination, the optical-ocular . . . ; in a certain sense it is the
> movement which is primary, and the sensation which is
> secondary, the movement of body, head and eye muscles
> determining the quality of what is experienced. [7]

Even this radically altered assessment of what is occurring tends to falsify the event, for the child is not simply looking at the candle and then deciding to reach for it but is from the outset seeing-to-reach:

> if this act, the seeing, stimulates another act, the reaching,
> it is because both of these acts fall within a larger coordination,
> because seeing and grasping have been so often bound together
> to reinforce each other, to help each other out, that each may
> be considered practically a subordinate member of a bigger
> coordination. [8]

After stipulating that the same analysis holds for what had been presented as the second "reflex arc" (the child being burned and withdrawing his hand), namely, that it is a sensorimotor coordination and not a mere sensation, Dewey declares that the reflex arc fails us in yet another way here. This second phase, the burn and the withdrawal, is more intimately a part of the first phase than the reflex-arc model could ever account for. The burn-withdrawal coordination

> is simply the completion, or fulfillment, of the previous
> eye-arm-hand coordination and not an entirely new occur-
> rence. Only because the heat-pain quale enters into the same
> circuit of experience with the optical-ocular and muscular
> quales, does the child learn from the experience and gain the
> ability to avoid the experience in the future. The so-called
> response is not merely *to* the stimulus; it is *into* it. The burn
> is original seeing, the original optical-ocular experience
> enlarged and transformed in its value. It is no longer mere
> seeing; it is seeing-of-a-light-that-means-pain-when-contact-
> occurs. [9]

In the place of a passive organism that had to be jolted into reactive response by some impression from an outside world or spurred into initiating activity by a power on a higher plane of existence, a soul or whatever, Dewey was constructing here a simple, naturalistic model of a human organism that had both these powers built into it—an organism that, in a word, both constituted its own experience and initiated its activity (in that it was inherently active). The reflex-arc idea,

> in its failure to see that the arc of which it talks is virtually a circuit, a continual reconstitution . . ., breaks continuity and leaves us nothing but a series of jerks, the origin of each jerk to be sought outside the process of experience itself, in either an external pressure of "environment," or else in an unaccountable spontaneous variation from within the "soul" or the "organism."

Or, looked at another way, the reflex arc

> still leaves us with sensation or peripheral stimulus; idea, or central process . . . ; and motor response, or act, as three disconnected existences, having to be somehow adjusted to each other, whether through the intervention of an extra-experimental soul, or by mechanical push and pull. [10]

After this brief excursion into its implications, Dewey returned to the circuit model itself, at pains again to impress on his readers how radical a reconceptualization of behavior he was suggesting. In thoroughly routinized, habitual activity, the thousands of small coordinations which make up the broad base of our behavior—putting on our gloves, walking, opening our front door—there is no such thing as a stimulus-response distinction:

> [Physically,] it is redistribution pure and simple, as much so as the burning of a log, or the falling of a house or the movement of the wind; [psychically,] there is simply a continuously ordered sequence of acts, all adapted in themselves and in the order of their sequence, to reach a certain objective end. . . . The end has got thoroughly organized into the means. In calling one stimulus, another response we mean nothing more than that such an orderly sequence of acts is taking place. [11]

What, then, of sensation and movement, stimulus and response? Don't we experience them? The answer is yes, but only when a particular set of circumstances occurs. When the action is already thoroughly coordinated, smooth and certain, there is no stimulus response as such.

But now take a child who, upon reaching for bright light (that is, exercising the seeing-reaching coordination) has sometimes had a delightful exercise, sometimes found something good to eat and sometimes burned himself. *Now the response is not only uncertain, but the stimulus is equally uncertain* . . .; it is precisely at this juncture and because of it that the distinction of sensation as stimulus and motion as response arises. [12]

The old coordination is called into question; the child must bring his attention to bear on the situation, he must decide what to do. There ensues, Dewey says, a sequence of acts something like the following. The child begins to experience anticipatory images of the various movements he might initiate and of their consequences. His attention becomes focused on the light, for the value and results of these possible movements are seen to depend on precisely what kind of light it is, on whether it is a glittering toy or a flame. When he has satisfied himself as to the nature of the light and the conditions he will have to meet to successfully complete the new coordination, the child then shifts his attention to the movement of his arm and the action he will take. [13]

In the first part of "The Reflex Arc Concept in Psychology" Dewey had suggested how man can be seen as an organism with a single pattern of activity that accounts satisfactorily for his entire experience. Here in the second part he in effect began to show how his hypothesis could be made to account for man as an organism that learns and grows. He was giving a naturalistic account of the origin of man's most "spiritual" activity, thinking.

Dewey's philosophy was now beginning to come into its maturity. In this period, the early 1890s, the Hegelianism had seen its purpose fulfilled and had gracefully slipped away. [14] Very much in the way it had for his teacher, George Sylvester Morris, it had served to assure Dewey that the universe is knowable, is properly home to man. As they saw it, Hume, Kant, and Spencer had each in his way closed the mind in on itself, while Hegel had left it free and puissant—puissant in that he gives a method of knowing the world. For Morris the method had been the traditional idealist analysis. For Dewey, as we have seen, it was psychology—declared as method in an abstract way in his articles in *Mind* in 1886, and later, in the 1890s, more concretely in "The Reflex Arc Concept in Psychology" and the work which led up to it.

∽

Ann Arbor
Dec 19 '91

MY DEAR HENRY
What do you think of the following for a simple and complete
view of the concept—consciousness turns back upon itself and
recognizes certain things as different and yet as the same—
draws thus a line about a number of objects which it yet in so
doing distinguishes as separate. Reasoning then becomes
simply the inclusion under a more general concept of two at
first unconnected ideas. . . . [15]

George Herbert Mead had been in the University of Michigan
department for a month when he was thus swept up in the spirit
of it ("a simple and complete view of the concept," "Reasoning
then becomes simply the inclusion . . .," etc.). These great cuts at
the most tangled of Gordian knots were oddly naive gestures to be
following four years of graduate study in the best universities, so
naive that one can't help but remark on their cathartic quality
and conclude again that Mead's professional training in philosophy and psychology had left his soul more than half-starved. His
second letter to Henry, written a week later, began immediately
with a diagram:

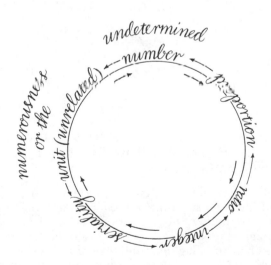

"This is one application of a great universe-formula of Dewey's," Mead explained, "an application to arithmetic."

> Starting with the undetermined number the first process in development is that of pure breaking up or analysis resulting in simple numerousness or the simple unit—unrelated; this reacts upon the undetermined number and gives as a result seriality that is the unit as in relation to those before and after itself. . . . [16]

Next, the circle again—this time as "applied to consciousness":

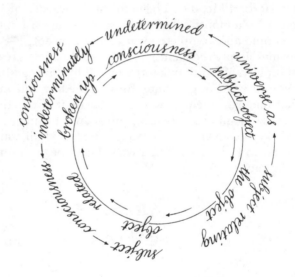

Words may have failed Mead at this point—his comment consisted of only a comparatively limp "This goes round again 3 times I believe." But the best was yet to come:

> Dewey called the scale a musical judgment and though he knows nothing of music, applied the formula—and struck [on the piano, presumably] the ratio of the scale and a number of other musical relations exactly. . . . This is only a suggestion of the thing. There are diagonals and several revolutions and applications on all sides—It applies beautifully to psychol-

ogy—All is going beautifully here. Come next May without fail.

> Yours most afftly,
> GEORGE

After he had suffered almost a decade of gloomy conviction that the universe is alien to man and impenetrable by his intellect, Mead could be pardoned for his excitement at seeing Dewey use his Hegelian formulas to *deduce*, no less, a musical scale. We may suspect he was bowled over altogether by Dewey's matter-of-fact acceptance of such congruences. Dewey, perhaps, accepted it with more composure; having spent five years arguing that the World is Mind, he may not have been too surprised to find out that indeed it is.

Mead's arrival at Michigan also coincided with Dewey's and Franklin Ford's last months of preparation for the publication of *Thought News*, and Mead was shortly rushing off a prospectus to Henry Castle, his erstwhile partner in another newspaper scheme:

> My DEAR HENRY,
> I am frightfully pushed trying to carry my work and absorb new ideas. I send what I know will be new life and inspiration—He [Ford] is no thinker. . . . He just offers himself to facts and they register themselves upon him when he has completed his struggle with them. He has wrestled wholly minded with the fact of organized intelligence—the meaning of Hegel—and the fact has succeeded in registering itself upon him.
> The thing is only the greatest that the world has ever seen. It is the sudden conscious recognition in an integral unit of society that he and all exist only as the expression of the universal self. [17]

In due course Mead sent Castle twenty-five copies of the announcement of *Thought News's* imminent appearance and instructions that he get his friends in Hawaii to subscribe. [18]

These first six months in Ann Arbor did not come down simply to a matter of Hegelian and Fordian excitements; the most important thing was what happened to Mead in himself. The reader will recall that, before he left Germany to go to Michigan, Mead had said how matters stood with him with regard both to his profession and to his hopes from life in general. The physiological psychology that he anticipated would be only a "drudgery" he would treat as a means to an end, and the end would be reform politics as a way of keeping out the night, as the only assertion man could make in a world without meaning for him. As for reconstructing the wholeness that his life had lost when he lost his religious faith—the surety, as he later put it, "that the world was ordered by some personal purpose whose result was assured, while the successful results of the lives of individual men and women depended largely upon their willingness to fit into this rational moral purpose"[19]—that possibility seemed to him gone beyond reclaiming.

Yet this is precisely what happened. As his first letters from Michigan indicated, he found Dewey to be the most convincing exponent of idealism he had ever encountered. What Dewey had over, say, Royce was not simply an occasional moment of wizardry at the piano keyboard but rather his feat of turning idealism from a dialectically argued system, such as Royce's or George Sylvester Morris's, into a system that was so intimately wrapped up with science. Mead had been through Harvard and the German universities, and this credential, of being "scientific," was now for him an absolute requisite if he were again to believe. But, that condition once granted, his capacity for faith was apparently undiminished. "I have at last reached a position I used to dream of in Harvard," he was later to write to Castle, "where it is possible at least to apply good straight phy psy to Hegel and I don't know what more a mortal can want on this earth."[20] When he was confronted by Dewey's message, Mead hesitated just for a moment and then rushed to embrace it. The fact that it was during this period that Dewey was rapidly converting the Hegelianism into what would eventually be known as instrumentalism was beside the point; what mattered was that Dewey's philosophy contained the saving news that Mead wanted to hear. In either guise its purport was the same: the universe is not an indifferent something out there. The World is Mind, and as mind it is meaning.

"Mr. Dewey is a man of not only great originality and profound thought, but the most appreciative thinker I ever met—I have gained more from him than from any one man I ever met."[21] Everything that had been bitter for Mead now turned sweet: "a philosophical education is a good thing because one loses the fear of ending up in bogs of bad 'isms.' One gets an unshakeable faith in a single reality to which all paths lead." [22]

"For the first time in my life has my thought assumed a definitely positive and cheerful aspect. I don't mean that there has been any break in it, but I have come to consciousness of the meaning of the faith that was in me, faith in the unity and meaning of life, and the absolute completeness of the statement which psychology can give."[23]

As this last remark would imply, Dewey had done even more than give Mead back his universe; he had also transformed for his new colleague the meaning of his discipline, physiological psychology. Mead had come to Ann Arbor with a great deal of personal detachment from the field; it had been a marriage of convenience for him, a second-best to pure philosophy, and he had been pessimistic about the chances of doing any significant research in it at such an out-of-the-way place as the University of Michigan. Dewey changed all that. How he did it should be clear. He introduced Mead to the work he was doing on the reflex-arc concept; he showed Mead how he was transforming the idealist assertion that the world is mind into its instrumentalist equivalent that all the questions of philosophy are to be studied through the type unit of human behavior (the "reflex arc," very soon to be corrected to the "reflex circuit"). Further, in an aspect of his thought that has not been stressed in this book, Dewey explained to Mead that a separation of mind and body had to be false procedure: the model of the boy reaching for the candle (particularly when the model was viewed in the light of Dewey's rethinking of it) showed that any notion that the *mind thought*, while the *body acted*, was unwarranted. Rather, the *organism behaved*: eye and arm and brain checked and reinforced one another in perfect democracy, brain being no more able to understand without the reach and touch of the arm than arm was able to function without eye.

Mead saw the implications of all this. Just as in 1885–86 Dewey had in an abstract sort of way declared the psychologist to be the modern philosopher, so he was now declaring the experimental and physiological psychologist to be the person best fitted to study "the unit of philosophy," the "type-action of the individual organism." Mead, who thought he had gone off into an ancillary discipline, found himself at center stage. At the end of that first year at Michigan, the Castle parents, now very old, offered to pay George's passage to a summer in Hawaii (Helen was already

there, apparently having left Ann Arbor sometime that spring).
Mead decided not to go.

MY DEAR FATHER AND MOTHER,
　　It has been a difficult and most trying decision that I have
had to make. It was practically balancing what I may do this
summer over against the probability of never meeting you. . . .
But I could not overlook what the summer might be to me or
rather to Helen and me. . . .
　　I have seen . . . that all matter, especially the human organism, becomes spiritual when one sees in it the processes of life
and thought, that the body and soul are but two sides of one
thing, and that the gulf between them is only the expression of
the fact that our life does not yet realize the ideal of what our
social life will be when our functions and acts shall be not
simply ours but the processes of the great body politic which is
God as revealed in the universe.
　　For me in Physiological Psychology the especial problem is to
recognize that our psychical life can all be read in the functions
of our bodies—that it is not the brain that thinks but our
organs in so far as they act together in the processes of life.
　　This is quite a new standpoint for the science and has a good
many important consequences—especially does it offer new
methods of experiment which must be worked out and I can't
do this if I do not have the summer here for study and the
arrangement of the laboratory. . . .
　　Please excuse this very abstract statement, but I wanted at
least just to indicate that my work here was not simply carrying
on technical labors to maintain myself in my position as
teacher and experimenter but that what I am at work on has
all the meaning of social and religious life in it. [24]

Put another way, Dewey's grand design, in which Mead was now
working, promised to invest in the person of the scientific
psychologist all those attributes and powers that in Mead's
childhood faith had resided in the philosopher-minister.

9   The Fruits of Pragmatism

The Mead we have seen in these pages was a vulnerable and impressionable person. He did not remain so, nor did he become simply an epigone of Dewey's. Rather, Dewey's (and Alfred North Whitehead's) final estimate of him, that Mead was "a seminal mind of the first order," is the accurate one. He adopted Dewey's construct but then developed it brilliantly in a direction of his own devising, arguing in a series of articles published over the next thirty years that man is social *before* he is individual, that our awareness of others precedes our awareness of ourselves, and that, indeed, certain aspects of our distinctively human behavior, particularly our consciousness of *meaning*, can be accounted for only if we accept the fact that man is an intrinsically social being.

This set of teachings resonated deeply within pragmatism. Dewey, for instance, turned to this social matrix as the context for man he had been searching for after he discarded Hegel's Universal Mind. Mead's "social self" resonated also outside instrumentalism and outside philosophy. His suggestions as to how man is socialized funded the young disciplines of social psychology and sociology with some of their most basic concepts: "role-playing," "the significant other," and so forth. Strange to say (given what we have seen of instrumentalism's beginnings), Mead's writings are probably more important in the intellectual world today than Dewey's are. If the fact is ironic, the reasons for it are more so. Mead meant his "social self" to be a reassuring teaching; its burden was that the individual, tamed from the outset, is willy-nilly a Progressive toiler for the common good ("the essentially social character of all conduct," he wrote; "... the recognition that all self-seeking has and must have a social end").[1] What has kept his thought in the forefront of modern social science, however, are the clinical and even sinister implications of the socializing mechanisms he wrote about: we are fascinated by how thoroughly we are conditioned by our social environment, how little we are creatures of our selves.

∽

As for John Dewey, the outlines of his career are well known. In 1894 he left Michigan for the University of Chicago. There he founded the Laboratory School and presided over the coterie of faculty and graduate students whom William James was to hail as "The Chicago School" upon the publication of their *Studies in Logical Theory* in 1903:

> Chicago University has . . . given birth to the fruit of its ten years of gestation under John Dewey. The result is wonderful—a *real school*, and *real thought*. Important thought, too! Did you ever hear of such a city or such a University? Here [at Harvard] we have thought, but no school. At Yale a school but no thought. Chicago has both.*

In 1904 Dewey quarreled with President Harper of the University of Chicago and resigned. Columbia University offered him a position, and he went to New York City, where he was to remain for the rest of his long and almost incredibly productive life. From his arrival there until his death in 1952 he wrote hundreds of articles and reviews and a dozen major books, all the while exploring that "flash of insight" he had had in his last years at Michigan. To understand the way Dewey developed his pragmatism and the use he made of it, it is necessary only to turn to any of the major books of philosophy he wrote in this period. *Experience and Nature*, however, the instrumentalist metaphysics which Dewey brought out in 1925, is particularly well suited for such a purpose.

---

*William James to Mrs. Henry Whitman, 29 October 1903, in Henry James, ed., *Letters of William James*, 2 vols. (Boston: Atlantic Monthly Press, 1920), 2:201–2. In his review of the book, James wrote: "Professor John Dewey, and at least ten of his disciples, have collectively put into the world a statement, homogeneous in spite of so many cooperating minds, of a view of the world, both theoretical and practical, which is so simple, massive, and positive that, in spite of the fact that many parts of it yet need to be worked out, it deserves the title of a new system of philosophy" (*Psychological Bulletin* 1 [January 1904]: 1).

Experience and Nature was unhurried and ruminative, in the characteristic style of the big books Dewey wrote in his maturity, and, again typically of Dewey, by turns felicitous and obscure in its presentation. "But although Dewey's book is incredibly ill written, it seemed to me after several rereadings to have a feeling of intimacy with the inside of the cosmos that I found unequaled. So methought God would have spoken had He been inarticulate but keenly desirous to tell you how it was."[2] Justice Holmes could rarely resist the temptation to be emphatic, but his praise does serve as a reminder of how remarkably winning a book *Experience and Nature* turned out to be. Quite as the young Dewey had hoped thirty years earlier, he had produced a relaxed and self-commending account of "the main standpoint, method, and categories of philosophy," one that might prove itself *"ambulando."* Gone was the tense and linear argumentation of his early writings, the straining to persuade his reader that the universe is Mind. Instrumentalism, or pragmatism, had absolved him of the need. Instead, he now dealt with "dualism"—its insistence on the fundamental gap between mind and matter—by a much more effective stratagem. He simply invited his audience to suspend these concerns, to begin thinking with him in the method of empirical naturalism and see what would result. This change in the reader's ways, he suggested, might "be hastened by calling attention to another context in which nature and experience get on harmoniously together—wherein experience presents itself as the method, and the only method, for getting at nature, penetrating its secrets, and wherein nature empirically disclosed ... deepens, enriches, and directs the further development of experience."[3] This other context, of course, was the natural sciences. The scientist does not worry about the competency of an empirical method to explore nature; he simply gets on with the work.

Dewey did likewise. After some preliminary discussion of method, he set about characterizing nature. It is an overlapping series of events, a congeries of comings-to-be and passings-out-of-existence. What we take to be immutable is only somewhat more permanent than what we know to be evanescent. Planets, mountains—all arrangements—had a beginning and will someday pass away. It is a universe of chance and impermanence; yet there occur certain outcomes which for man "have the value of consummation and fulfillment."[4] The only way to assure their presence is "by ability to control the changes that intervene between the beginning and the end of a process. These intervening terms when brought under control are *means* in the literal and in the practical sense of the word. When mastered in actual experience they constitute tools, techniques, mechanisms." [5]

It should be noticed that, after his initial brief account of nature, Dewey moved immediately into the problems of the conduct of human life in such a universe. This was fair warning of what the rest of the book would be like. The reviewers complained that Dewey's venture advertised itself as a metaphysics ("To discover some of these general features of experienced things and to interpret their significance for a philosophic theory of the universe in which we live is the aim of this volume")[6] but that, precisely as a metaphysics, it delivered very little. *Experience and Nature* was a book about experience, but "we *have* experience and we want to *know* what nature is," one critic grumbled. [7]

What Dewey's response would have been is easy to guess. From his earliest gibes at Herbert Spencer's "unknowable" he had been firm on this point. To talk of anything as outside experience is absurd. We have nothing but experience; what isn't in experience is nowhere. Yet his apparent firmness did not shield Dewey from the charge that would always dog his philosophy: that he was having it both ways. If experience is all, did not the very title of his book invite misunderstanding? And his chapter titles, with their apparent promise of commerce between subjective and objective—"Nature, Means and Knowledge," "Nature, Mind and the Subject," and so forth—did they not also invite misunderstanding? If Dewey had written simply as a dualist, confessing a world out there and a mind in here, these titles would have been unobjectionable; even if he had held consistently to a position that nature is in some way a phase within experience, they would have been unobjectionable. But he didn't do either of these things, he did both.

The book was in the main about experience, how man constitutes and behaves in his environment; however, at frequent and important junctures Dewey did rely on the idea of an independent world, external to experience. George P. Adams, the philosopher who reviewed *Experience and Nature* for the *Inter-*

national Journal of Ethics, in some exasperation began to ambush Dewey, catching him where he saw him referring to a region independent of experience. "The visible is set in the invisible," he found Dewey writing, "and in the end what is unseen decides what happens in the seen; the tangible rests precariously upon the untouched and ungrasped." Adams asked: "Does this contrast occur *within* experience, or is it a contrast between what is within experience and something outlying? If the former, are we to be said to see the invisible, to touch the intangible, to grasp the ungrasped? If the latter, does not experience become a sub-stantive region set over against an environing world of the nature of things?"[8] In another place Adams found H_2O described as embodying in its essence "instrumental efficiency in respect to things independent of human affairs" and he put the same challenge: "to have discovered *any* feature or structure of things 'independent of human affairs' would seem to be an instance of a kind of insight into the real texture of things, an instance of knowledge of the sort which has been repudiated."[9]

These instances that Adams tracked down were only that: instances. But it could be said that Dewey's whole structure in *Experience and Nature* was based on his initial characterization of nature as a series of events. It was a brief and informal metaphysic, but the book could not have begun without it; his establishment of certain truths about nature freed him to write a book about human behavior.

Experience and Nature is in fact very much a psychology. Those chapters with their curiously opaque titles—"Nature, Mind and the Subject," "Nature, Life and Body-Mind," "Exis-tence, Ideas and Consciousness"—turn out to be a phenome-nology of man's reaction to his environment and an analysis of the way man organizes himself in order to wrest from the environ-ment the ends he values. Dewey followed human experience as it encounters nature, comes to value certain ends and consumma-tions, fashions instruments to attain them, turns to reflection in problematic situations, and through communication with other men learns to assign meanings to existence. Man becomes thereby *Homo sapiens*, the creature who has intelligence, who can think in universals, think hypothetically, abstract from the immediate situation and combine and recombine ideas, and then return to nature vastly more able to manipulate it and appreciate it.

There are history and anthropology in *Experience and Nature* also; and, not surprisingly, the hero of the piece is scientific man, the latecomer who at last fully frees our powers. But mostly there is psychology, disarmingly informal and discursive. The book contains long sections on Dewey's most basic insight, that the beginnings of thought are to be found in problematic situations; a fine summary of Mead's and Dewey's derivation of man's intelligence from his sociality; and discussion of how man comes to value certain things in experience. By any criterion, it is remarkably good psychology, and Holmes's estimate that the book possessed an unequaled "feeling of intimacy with the inside of the cosmos" does not seem so much of an exaggeration.

By the time *Experience and Nature* was written, Dewey's philosophy had grown. One senses that Dewey had absorbed the criticisms that had been leveled at it over the years: that in its concentration on perfecting a model of human *activity*, pragmatism or instrumentalism had paid too little attention to man's original, direct, qualitative contact with his surroundings, and that, as critic after critic had complained, man seeks more than simply "instrumental" ends—he is a contemplator also, and an enjoyer. Accordingly, much of what was new in *Experience and Nature* was there to *ground* human activity, so to speak, in the immediately felt qualities of things and in consummatory, as distinguished from instrumental, values. There is room for argument on how legitimately these considerations can logically be integrated into an instrumentalist system, but the effect of their presence on *Experience and Nature* as a cultural artifact, as a book, was entirely salutary. They tended to free a very intelligent man to talk about human nature without having to reduce behavior to some original, too-simple unit. Instrumentalism in its original form had already been a comparatively mild master to Dewey in this way; after all, it attributed complexity and some real interiority to human psychology (unlike Watsonian behaviorism, for instance), and it portrayed a self-actualizing, self-regulating organism. Now it freed Dewey thoroughly, letting him be as large-minded, receptive, and constructive as he might be. It was this, finally, that the reviewers of *Experience and Nature* were delighted by. The book, it should be remembered, was a long one, over four hundred pages, and there was a great deal of room in it for a sort of generalized and old-fashioned wisdom. For pages at a time the reader found himself following a leisurely Dewey down one bypath or another, the little excursion nicely done—the philosophy not so elegant as a Santayana's, nor so suffused with personality as William James's, but wonderfully intelligent and concerned—and surprisingly worldly.

The Dewey who wrote *Experience and Nature* had been in New York on the Columbia University faculty for twenty years and in Chicago for the ten years before that. The cities and the urbanity of the two great universities had changed him; it was symbolic that the first thing Dewey had done on being appointed to the University of Chicago in 1894 was to visit the Columbian Exposition. His post at that university had also brought him within range of Thorstein Veblen, and Veblen's mark is easy to see in *Experience and Nature*. Then at Columbia one of Dewey's first graduate students (and apparently the one he was closest to in the early years there) had been Max Eastman, a commuter for four years between Greenwich Village and Dewey's study in Morningside Heights. Several years later, in 1916 and 1917, Dewey had cooperated with that band of critics of the American culture who founded the *Seven Arts* magazine, and a year or two after that his intense relationship began with Albert Barnes and the Philadelphia millionaire's magnificent collection of modern French art. By the time he wrote *Experience and Nature* he was reading widely in anthropology and cultural anthropology. He smoked now, and he liked a drink.

It is hard to imagine the sober young Progressive at Michigan beginning a chapter as Dewey did in New York in the 1920s:

> Human experience in the large, in its course and conspicuous features, has for one of its most striking features preoccupation with direct enjoyment, feasting and festivities; ornamentation, dance, song, dramatic pantomime, telling yarns and enacting stories. In comparison with intellectual and moral endeavor, this trait of experience has hardly received the attention from philosophers that it demands. Even philosophers who have conceived that pleasure is the sole motive of man and the attainment of happiness his whole aim, have given a curiously sober, drab, account of the working of pleasure and the search for happiness. Consider the utilitarians how they toiled, spun and wove, but who never saw man arrayed in joy as the lilies of the field. Happiness was to

them a matter of calculation and effort, of industry guided by mathematical book-keeping. The history of man shows however that man takes his enjoyment neat, and at as short range as possible.

Direct appropriations and satisfactions were prior to anything but the most elementary and exigent prudence, just as the useful arts preceded the sciences. The body is decked before it is clothed. While homes are still hovels, temples and palaces are embellished. Luxuries prevail over necessities except when necessities can be festally celebrated. Men make a game of their fishing and hunting, and turn to the periodic and disciplinary labor of agriculture only when inferiors, women and slaves, cannot be had to do the work. [10]

∽

When he wrote *Experience and Nature* Dewey was in his early and middle sixties. The book is a considerable tribute to the quality of his maturity. His optimism is somewhat chastened (as should be apparent from the paragraphs quoted above), and he is far more vividly aware of man's capacity for self-defeat. But the fundamental quality still is energy and steady hope. Dewey was blessed with good health—he had more than a quarter-century of productive work yet before him—and the tone of his book is in part a reflection of this mundane fact; but it is much more a tribute to his philosophy and to his disposition and psychic integrity. All of the intellectual and productive giants with whom Dewey's career is closely associated were afflicted with one or another trouble of the spirit: Mead, James, Veblen, Santayana, Bertrand Russell, even G. Stanley Hall. [11] Dewey alone was exempt. No crabbiness, no *idées fixes*, no discernible fatigue, no alienation.

That he remained a significant figure in American intellectual life is well known. Indeed, his importance was hardly lessened when, after the first third of the twentieth century, American academic philosophers were grazing elsewhere in newer empiricisms and in linguistic philosophy. This diminishment of technical interest in instrumentalism would leave untouched the institutionalization of his educational ideas in the teachers colleges, an enormously important focus in American education.

And it would not change the fact that in the 1920s and 1930s, two decades in which social planning and administration were the predominant interest of America's liberal intelligentsia, Dewey's works were a bible, turned to for inspiration, justification, morale, philosophy. He wrote pieces specifically about these problems, most notably *The Public and Its Problems* (1927) and articles such as the 1931 "Social Science and Social Control," with its rousing conclusion:

> I am not arguing here for the desirability of social planning and control. That is another question. Those who are satisfied with present conditions and who are hopeful of turning them to account for personal profit and power will answer it in the negative. What I am saying is that if we want something to which the name "social science" may be given, there is only one way to go about it, namely, by entering upon the path of social planning and control. Observing, collecting, recording and filing tomes of special phenomena without deliberately trying to do something to bring a desired state of society into existence only encourages a conflict of opinion and dogma in their interpretation. If the social situation out of which these facts emerge is itself confused and chaotic because it expresses socially unregulated purpose and haphazard private intent, the facts themselves will be confused, and we shall add only intellectual confusion to practical disorder. When we deliberately employ whatever skill we possess in order to serve the ends which we desire, we shall begin to attain a measure of at least intellectual order and understanding. And if past history teaches anything, it is that with intellectual order we have the surest possible promise of advancement to practical order. [12]

But we need not turn to such topical writings to find this focus in Dewey; with George Adams we can see in *Experience and Nature*, not really a metaphysics, but "an inquiry into the nature of human goods and meanings and the possibility of their intelligent liberation and control." [13]

Dewey's importance to these groups of people, appropriately dubbed "the service intellectuals"—reforming bureaucrats, professional educators, all those professionally engaged in the distribution of social services in twentieth-century America—formed one great arm of his influence. The other was equally general.

From the 1880s until approximately 1910 the institution of the university was the locus par excellence of American intellectual activity. This picture changed when, toward the end of the first decade of the new century, there sprang up—quite suddenly, really—a host of other intellectual enterprises, most notably an array of serious magazines, in which a new generation of the intelligentsia made their careers. Max Eastman in the *New Masses*, Walter Lippmann in the *New Republic*, Randolph Bourne and the *Seven Arts*: these are famous pairings, and the list could be extended. Generally speaking, these people had been born in the 1880s, had attended major eastern universities (Harvard and Columbia), and then around 1910 had left to make lives for themselves as social critics, founding and editing new journals as vehicles for their ideas. Although they characteristically did not make their careers in the universities, they had funded their thought there. Their essays and books in the period through the First World War referred frequently to the older men who had taught them: George Santayana, Charles A. Beard, James Harvey Robinson, William James, and John Dewey. [14]

The young critics invoked these last two names more than any others— "James and Dewey offered the nearest American model for the kind of generalizing language they required."[15] The two philosophers were rewarded not just for being in the most universal of academic disciplines but for keeping to its summit, where they could survey and speak to all sides of human affairs. James's and Dewey's far-ranging ways and their resistance to getting completely absorbed in the technical discussions of professional philosophy would bring them rough treatment at the hands of other philosophers, seeking unequivocal language and testable propositions; but it kept their philosophies accessible and important to other publics. Dewey's message, particularly, was an appealing one to creative young people, beginning to feel their own adult powers, at the outset of their careers. His philosophy is about life's possibilities and the validity of individual experience. It is a secular philosophy. It gives short shrift to received norms and does not tarry long over life's tragedies. Dewey's philosophy appealed, also, for subtler, more circumstantial reasons. Eastman, Bourne, Lippmann, Van Wyck Brooks, Waldo Frank, Edmund Wilson, all those young people who found their way to New York's intellectual circles around the year 1910, had in common an ideal of cultural nationalism. For a good ten years their various works reflected a determination that America as a civilization should at last discover its own truest meaning and give it worthy creative expression. There had always been an element of this in Dewey, also; it was not precisely a cultural nationalism, but a commitment to America as a democracy and a conviction that there was a close affinity between democracy and his way of doing philosophy. It took little straining to derive from his writings a program of cultural revolution and reconstruction for America; the arenas were to be the education of our children, our ethics, and, most diffuse of all, "the way we think."

In their well-founded enthusiasm for Dewey's ideas on these subjects, these young critics failed to notice that Dewey had very little to say about politics. They were happy to take him as they found him, a thinker who wanted to set free our powers. They quoted him on the death of dogmas, on the need for "scientific" problem-solving, on the great potential of a reformed education, and on the hopefulness of the new age.

But events caught up with the critics, and many of them— Eastman, Edmund Wilson, Randolph Bourne—eventually *were* drawn into politics; they found themselves facing the First World War and its implications, the more abiding conditions of social injustice, and even the very general issue of the resistance of America as a civilization to the deep cultural changes they were proposing to it. Much more urgently than ever before, they were forced to consider questions about economic and political power in the United States. By reflex they turned again to Dewey's thought, but they gained little this time, finding that his vaunted "method of creative intelligence" yielded no special insights into these national troubles.

The most dramatic such shock of recognition was Randolph Bourne's. A young critic, a champion especially of Dewey's educational ideas, Bourne in 1917 was outraged to see Dewey support America's entry into the war and take to scolding pacifists and war resisters. The essays Bourne published in the *Seven Arts* denouncing this choice of Dewey's are among the classics of American denunciatory prose. In "Twilight of Idols" Bourne wrote:

Dewey's philosophy is inspiring enough for a society at peace, prosperous and with a fund of progressive good will. It is a philosophy of hope, of clear-sighted comprehension of materials and means. Where institutions are at all malleable, it is the only clue for improvement. It is scientific method applied to "uplift." But this careful adaptation of means to desired ends, this experimental working out of control over brute forces and dead matter in the interests of communal life, depends on a store of rationality, and is effective only where there is strong desire for progress. [16]

Now, however, these circumstances had fled, and the declared national purpose was war; pragmatism's root ideal was "adjustment to your situation, in radiant cooperation with reality," and its success was "likely to be just that and no more." [17] The war effort was the situation, the "reality," and Dewey's philosophy was incapable of criticism or of proposing a counterideal.

"Twilight of Idols" was not a neat or entirely coherent essay, and this rawness lent poignancy to its discoveries. [18] "How could the pragmatist mind accept war without more violent protest, without a greater wrench?" "A philosopher who senses so little the sinister forces of war, who is so much more concerned over the excesses of the pacifists than over the excesses of military policy, who can feel only amusement at the idea that anyone should try to conscript thought, who assumes that the war-technique can be used without trailing along with it the mob-fanaticisms, the injustices and hatreds, that are organically bound up with it, is speaking to another element of the younger intelligentsia than that to which I belong." Dewey's allies "are all hostile to impossibilism, to apathy, to any attitude that is not a cheerful and brisk setting to work to use the emergency to consolidate the gains to democracy. Not, Is it being used? but, Let us make a flutter about using it!" [19]

The war has revealed a younger intelligentsia, trained up in the pragmatic dispensation, immensely ready for the executive ordering of events, pitifully unprepared for the intellectual interpretation or the idealistic focussing of ends. The young men in Belgium, the officer's training corps, the young men being sucked into the councils at Washington and into war-organization everywhere, have among them a definite element, upon whom Dewey, as veteran philosopher, might well bestow a papal blessing. They have absorbed the secret of scientific method as applied to political administration. They are liberal, enlightened, aware. They are touched with creative intelligence toward the solution of political and industrial problems. . . .

There seems to have been a peculiar congeniality between the war and these men. It is as if the war and they had been waiting for each other. One wonders what scope they would have had for their intelligence without it. Probably most of them would have gone into industry and devoted themselves to sane reorganization schemes. What is significant is that it is the technical side of the war that appeals to them, not the interpretive or political side. The formulation of values and ideals, the production of articulate and suggestive thinking, had not, in their education, kept pace, to any extent whatever, with their technical aptitude. . . .

It is true, Dewey calls for a more attentive formulation of war-purposes and ideas, but he calls largely to deaf ears. His disciples have learned all too literally the instrumental attitude toward life, and, being immensely intelligent and energetic, they are making themselves efficient instruments of the war-technique, accepting with little question the ends as announced from above. [20]

Bourne's belated realization that there had been *two* types of people sitting in Dewey's classrooms—cultural radicals like himself and the friends who had worked with him on the *Columbia Monthly*, and this other lot, those future administrative careerists—was an important moment in American intellectual life, the end of an enthusiasm. ("To those of us who have taken Dewey's philosophy almost as our American religion, it never occurred that values could be subordinated to technique.") [21] Bourne's anger at Dewey was brilliant. Though his own prescriptions for his America are vague enough—he wanted a Nietzschean "transvaluation of values"—Bourne elucidated the weaknesses in the instrumental outlook in a way that has hardly been surpassed since: "there was always that unhappy ambiguity in [Dewey's] doctrine as to just how values were created, and it became easier and easier to assume that just any growth was justified and almost any activity valuable so long as it achieved ends." [22]

This said, though, several rejoinders are in order. The "unhappy ambiguity" in Dewey's philosophy as to how values are created was not Dewey's problem alone; it haunts any philosophy that does not allow itself to appeal to some transcendent source—which is only to say that the problem troubles most of modern thought. Second, if Bourne was right and Dewey's natural constituency was indeed "earnest . . . young liberals"—the Delos Wilcoxes and Frank Mannys and their twentieth-century counterparts, "prudent, enlightened college men" bent on careers in education and public administration—then why was Bourne himself so attracted to Dewey? And Max Eastman, and, later on, people as diverse and different from each other as Sidney Hook and the romantics of educational reform in the 1960s? None of these fit the stereotype, and yet Dewey fascinated and inspired them all. Of course there were historical circumstances which help to account for these successive waves, but in each instance the question can be fully answered only by recalling that Dewey was an unusual combination of two strengths. The promulgator of instrumentalism, the philosopher who energetically and faithfully worked at his system, was joined to another man, the Dewey who was so delighted with William James's 1890 *Psychology* and was teaching it to his students a bare month or two after he received it. This other Dewey was as receptive as the first was single-minded. His philosophy originally was too sober; he loosened it and let some irony into it. It didn't have an aesthetic; he wrote *Art as Experience*. It needed its logic; he brought that out when he was almost eighty. After Versailles Dewey saw that he had been wrong about the World War; in the early 1930s he was to be found to the left of Roosevelt's Democratic Party; later in that decade he presided over the inquiry into Stalin's slander of Trotsky; and in the early 1950s, when he was in his nineties, he was rallying his younger friends against Joseph McCarthy. This has been a book about openness and growth; it would be appropriate for it to end on that note.

Notes

1. Early Years

1. The standard sources on Dewey's youth are Jane Dewey, ed., "Biography of John Dewey," in Paul Arthur Schilpp, ed., *The Philosophy of John Dewey* (Evanston and Chicago: Northwestern University Press, 1939); John Dewey, "From Absolutism to Experimentalism," in George P. Adams and William P. Montague, eds., *Contemporary American Philosophy*, 2 vols. (New York: Macmillan, 1930), 2:13–27; George Dykhuizen, *The Life and Mind of John Dewey* (Carbondale: Southern Illinois University Press, 1973). Unless otherwise indicated, the factual material in the account of Dewey's boyhood in this chapter is drawn from these sources. The emphases and interpretation are of course my own.

2. Sidney Hook, "Some Memories of John Dewey," *Commentary* 14 (September 1952): 246.

3. Lucina Dewey, George Dykhuizen has found, was portrayed under the name "Mrs. Carver" as counselor of college men in a novel, *Freshman and Senior* (Boston, 1899), by one Elvirton Wright. The book was a publication of the Congregational Sunday-School and Publishing Society. See Dykhuizen, *Life and Mind of John Dewey*, p. 7.

4. Quoted in Dykhuizen, *Life and Mind of John Dewey*, p. 6.

5. Dewey, "From Absolutism to Experimentalism," p. 19.

6. Jane Dewey, ed., "Biography of John Dewey," pp. 6–7.

7. Dewey, "From Absolutism to Experimentalism," p. 13.

8. See Lewis Feuer, "John Dewey's Reading at College," *Journal of the History of Ideas* 19 (June 1958): 415–21.

9. Years later he recalled that it was about this time that he first "tried to work up a little affair" with a girl—a cousin of his. "I thought something ought to be done. But I couldn't do it. I was too bashful. I was abnormally bashful. I was abnormal" (Max Eastman, "John Dewey," *Atlantic* 168 [1941]: 672–73).

10. Ibid., p. 673.

11. Dewey to W. T. Harris, 17 May 1881, quoted in Dykhuizen, *Life and Mind of John Dewey*, p. 23.

12. Ibid., p. 25.

13. See *In Memoriam Henry A. P. Torrey, LL.D.* (Burlington: University of Vermont, 1906); John Wright Buckham, "A Group of American Idealists," *Personalist* 1 (April 1920): 18–31; Lewis Feuer, "H. A. P. Torrey and John Dewey," *American Quarterly* 10 (1958): 34–54.

14. Buckham, "A Group of American Idealists," p. 24.

15. Edward H. Griffin, "Address of Rev. Dr. Griffin," in *In Memoriam H. A. P. Torrey*, p. 12. The phrasing of this description may possibly indicate that Torrey was enough of a Kantian not to claim an out-and-out *metaphysical* intuition, when he could avoid it, but only an intuition into the "character and meaning" of things for man.

16. John Wright Buckham, "Professor Torrey as Thinker and Teacher," in *In Memoriam H. A. P. Torrey*, p. 30.

17. Lewis Feuer, "H. A. P. Torrey and John Dewey," p. 42.

18. Dewey, "From Absolutism to Experimentalism," pp. 14–15.

19. Buckham, "A Group of American Idealists," p. 24.

20. Dewey, "From Absolutism to Experimentalism," p. 14.

21. Dewey to W. T. Harris, 22 October 1881, quoted in Dykhuizen, *Life and Mind of John Dewey*, p. 24.

22. Torrey to George Sylvester Morris, 11 February 1882, Special Collections, Milton S. Eisenhower Library, The Johns Hopkins University, Baltimore. Quoted in Dykhuizen, *Life and Mind of John Dewey*, p. 26.

2. Morris and Hall

1. Robert Mark Wenley, *The Life and Work of George Sylvester Morris* (New York: Macmillan, 1917), passim.

2. Ibid., pp. 206–7, 228 ff. See also letters from Union classmates of Morris's written to Wenley when he was collecting material for the Morris biography (Michigan Historical Collections, George Sylvester Morris Papers). There is extant no direct reference to the matter by Morris himself. Wenley concluded: "save for confidences imparted to one or two friends, he left no evidence of the trial through which he went between 1868 and 1873. We know that it drove him in upon himself, to such an extent as to affect his personal relations with others, even with his young students, who judged him strange or 'queer.' 'The rest is silence' " (p. 228).

3. Quoted ibid., p. 116.

4. Ibid., p. 118.

5. Ibid., p. 128.

6. George Sylvester Morris, "Friedrich Adolf Trendelenburg," *New Englander* 33 (1874): 287–336.

7. Ibid., p. 321.

8. Ibid., p. 323.

9. Morris, "The Philosophy of Art," *Journal of Speculative Philosophy* 10 (1876): 13. Three years earlier, when he had been memorializing the latter-day Aristotelianism of Trendelenburg, Morris had seen it differently:

No one is angry with the eye when it acts with the unexpressed consciousness that the realm of its activity is not that of unchanging, pure light, but of light that is modified, reflected or refracted in the various plays of color, that it lives not in the brightness of the sun in the heavens, but in the sphere of terrestrial light. But human thought is [wrongfully] reproached with incredulity or indolence, when, like the eye, it knows that the circle of the finite and conditioned, which is surely broad enough is the limit of its free and joyous activity. ["Trendelenburg," p. 328.]

10. Morris, "The Immortality of the Human Soul," *Bibliotheca Sacra* 33 (1876): 715.

11. "Trendelenburg," p. 332.

12. Morris, "The Final Cause as Principle of Cognition in Nature," *Journal of the Transactions of the Victoria Institute* 9 (1875): 176-204, and "The Theory of Unconscious Intelligence as Opposed to Theism," ibid. 11 (1876): 247-91. Both papers show the influence of Trendelenburg, but, as Wenley characterized them:

> The emphasis here laid upon the inevitable collision between natural science and spiritual aspiration, is pushed very nigh the point where an opposition within experience becomes irremediable, producing an external separation or dualism between intelligence and belief. For this reason, Morris does not wave science aside. He takes the simple course of staking off a claim for it. As for the spiritual aspirations, however, they must find satisfaction in that 'solemn shadow-land of unchangeable ideas,' the Unconditioned. [Wenley, *Life and Work of George Sylvester Morris*, p. 243.]

13. R. L. Nettleship, ed., *Works of Thomas Hill Green* (London: Longmans, Green & Co., 1890), vol. 1. The two works, entitled, respectively, *Introduction to Hume's Treatise of Human Nature* and *Mr. Herbert Spencer and Mr. G. H. Lewes: Their Application of the Doctrine of Evolution to Thought*, compose all but the last few pages of the 541-page first volume.

14. *British Thought and Thinkers* (1880); *Kant's Critique of Pure Reason* (1882); *Philosophy and Christianity* (1883); and *Hegel's Philosophy of the State and of History* (1887).

15. John Dewey, "The Philosophy of Thomas Hill Green," *Andover Review* 11 (April 1889): 335-55. This article is reprinted in Jo Ann Boydston, ed., *The Early Works of John Dewey, 1882-1898*, 5 vols. (Carbondale: Southern Illinois University Press, 1967-72), 3:14-35. Henceforth, references to this definitive edition will be given as, e.g., *EW* 3, pp. 14-35. My summary of Green's philosophy follows Dewey's in his article. See also Melvin Richter, *The Politics of Conscience: T. H. Green and His Age* (Cambridge: Harvard University Press, 1964).

16. Dewey, "The Philosophy of Thomas Hill Green," *EW* 3, p. 20.

17. Ibid., p. 22.

18. Ibid.

19. Ibid., p. 17.

20. Morris, *Hegel's Philosophy of the State and of History* (Chicago: S. C. Griggs & Co., 1887), pp. 292-93.

21. Ibid., p. 235.

22. Untitled typed lecture notes for a course on political philosophy, pp. 32-33, in George Sylvester Morris Papers, Michigan Historical Collections, Ann Arbor.

23. Typed lecture notes for a course titled "Real Logic," p. 15 (Morris Papers). It should be noted that Morris did not become exclusively a neo-Hegelian but combined this structure with many of Trendelenburg's doctrines; his "developed" philosophy was a melange of the two: he retained the Aristotelian tenet that the world really exists apart from mind, but he relied on the Hegelianism to establish that its *meaning* is for mind.

24. In each of the first two years of his connection with Hopkins, 1878 and

1879, Morris spent one month in Baltimore, giving a set of twenty public lectures; during each of the following three years he was in residence for three months.

25. Granville Stanley Hall, *Life and Confessions of a Psychologist* (New York: Appleton, 1923), pp. 149–50. This book, Hall's autobiography, must be used with caution. There is, however, an excellent definitive biography by Dorothy Ross, *G. Stanley Hall: The Psychologist as Prophet* (Chicago: University of Chicago Press, 1972).

26. Hall, *Life and Confessions*, p. 196.

27. Ibid., pp. 207–8.

28. Ibid., p. 215. Hall's choice was a shrewd one. As part of his explanation of why Morris lost out to Hall, Wenley said of Gilman, " 'Pedagogics' he could decry, with an eye to administration; deduction of the categories left him helpless" (Wenley, *Life and Work of George Sylvester Morris*, p. 151).

29. Hall, *Life and Confessions*, p. 216.

30. Hall had kind words for Smith, who suggested to him "just the right reading at the right time" and advised him to go to Europe. Beecher asked Hall whether his theological studies at Union had made him "more or less devout." Hall answered "less," and Beecher admitted him into his church, commending him for his honesty.

See Hall's description of Trendelenburg's mannerisms (*Life and Confessions*, pp. 190–91) and Hall's decisions to forgo attending the lectures of theologians and philosophers of the stature of Zeller and Lotze (ibid., p. 210). As for Hegelianism, Hall wrote to William James that he thought it "unsurpassed for helping men easily and without agony or crisis over any part of the long way from Rome to reason, but to rest in it as a finality is arrested development, and to go back to it seems to me mystic and retrogressive" (letter of 15 February 1880, quoted in Ralph Barton Perry, *The Thought and Character of William James*, 2 vols. [Boston: Little, Brown & Co., 1935], 2:21).

3. Dewey at Hopkins

1. George Dykhuizen, *The Life and Mind of John Dewey*, pp. 28 ff. (see chap. 1, n. 1).

2. Ibid. The address was published in volume 18 (January 1883) of the *Journal of Speculative Philosophy* under its original title; it is reprinted in *EW 1*, pp. 19–33.

3. See above, chap. 2.

4. Dewey, "From Absolutism to Experimentalism," p. 19 (see chap. 1, n. 1).

5. When Morris died in 1889, Dewey couched a eulogy of Morris, which he wrote for a student publication at Michigan, in a familiar rhetoric, one that shows better than anything else that Dewey saw in Morris the same type of cultural figure he had seen in Torrey. Morris, he said,

> was preëminently a man in whom those internal divisions, which eat into the heart of so much of contemporary spiritual life, and which rob the intellect of its faith in truth, and the will of its belief in the value of life, had been overcome. In the philosophical and religious conviction of the unity of man's spirit with the divine he had that rest which is energy. This wholeness of

intelligence and will was the source of the power, the inspiring power, of his life. . . . There was nothing in him which he held as his own: he had made the great renunciation. [*Palladium* 31 (1889): 110–18; *EW 3*, pp. 3–13.]

6. See, for instance, Dewey's "The Philosophy of Thomas Hill Green," *Andover Review* 11 (April 1889): 337–55; *EW 3*, pp. 14–35.

7. Dewey to H. A. P. Torrey, 14 February 1883, quoted in Dykhuizen, *Life and Mind of John Dewey*, p. 31.

8. The article appeared in the April 1884 issue of the *Journal*, vol. 18, pp. 162–74; *EW 1*, pp. 34–47.

9. Dewey to W. T. Harris, 17 January 1884, W. T. Harris Papers, House Library, University of Southern California, Los Angeles. Quoted in Dykhuizen, *Life and Mind of John Dewey*, p. 30.

10. Ibid.

11. George Sylvester Morris, "The Philosophy of the State and of History," in G. S. Hall, ed., *Pedagogical Library*, vol. 1: *Methods of Teaching History*, 2d ed. (Boston: D. C. Heath & Co., 1886), pp. 150–51.

12. Dewey to W. T. Harris, 17 January 1884, W. T. Harris Papers.

13. Ibid.; quoted in Dykhuizen, *Life and Mind of John Dewey*, p. 37. Dewey's dissertation has been lost.

14. Dewey, "From Absolutism to Experimentalism," p. 15.

15. Dewey, "The New Psychology," *Andover Review* 2 (1884): 278–89; *EW 1*, pp. 48–60.

16. Ibid., *EW 1*, p. 60 (the end of the article).

17. As far as I know, Dewey never acknowledged Smyth or for that matter even mentioned his name. I came across him by accident: reading "The New Psychology" within a few days after seeing Smyth's article "The Dynamical Theory of the Intuitions" listed in the table of contents of the *New Englander*, I remembered the expression and looked into it. Dewey, I think, actually forgot Smyth (for reasons which I go into in chapter 4) soon after he used him.

18. Newman Smyth, *Recollections and Reflections* (New York: Scribner's, 1926), passim. Smyth also contributed "a brief narrative of the progress of his thought and experience" to John Wright Buckham's *Progressive Religious Thought in America* (Boston, 1919). The reader will remember Buckham as Dewey's boyhood friend.

Smyth was a really lovely man. His autobiography could serve as the archetype of a whole group of New Englanders of his generation: the town boyhood, local schooling, and then a New England college or seminary, the Civil War experience, the crisis with skepticism born of a too abstract religion. Then Germany (almost invariably Berlin and Halle, because of their orthodoxy and their American connections of the previous generation, men such as Henry Boynton Smith of the Union Theological Faculty), and the rebirth of faith and its liberalization. Then home and a life of service, with "humanity" and "development" as its watchwords. To give some idea of the magic of the concept of evolution or development in the German theological scene, Smyth told the story of Tholuck that "Once . . . he suddenly stopped . . . and threw this question out at a student walking with him: 'Why did not the Almighty strike the devil dead?' The youth immediately replied: 'Because, I suppose he wanted to see how the creature would develop' " (*Recollections and Reflections*, p. 90). In later years,

Smyth tried to make American Protestants aware of the Catholic Modernists and of the hope he saw in that movement for the eventual reunion of the Christian churches. He even learned Italian so that he could read the Modernist literature and correspond with its leaders. Toward the end of his life he was one of the leaders in ecumenism and was a principal founder of the World Council of Churches. Much of Smyth's theology is as fresh and attractive today as it was when he wrote it. See, for example, his second book, based on his early sermons, *Old Faiths in New Light* (New York: Scribner's, 1879).

19. Smyth, "The Dynamical Theory of the Intuitions," *New Englander* 37 (1878): 353–61; "Orthodox Rationalism," *Princeton Review* n.s. 9 (1882): 294–312; "Professor Harris's Contribution to Theism," *Andover Review* 1 (1884): 132–48; "Samuel Harris, *The Religious Feeling*" (review article), *New Englander* 37 (1878): 72–79.

20. "Our belief in God, then, is not merely the end of a series of logical probabilities; it is not a startled leap of faith from the world as a finite premise to God as an infinite conclusion—all reasoning from nature up to God, if God is not first in our thoughts, involves either false logic or a pseudo-Infinite" (Smyth, "Orthodox Rationalism," p. 300). It should in fairness be noted that the Scottish argument for the existence of God is not as thin as it looks in transcription. In its subtler forms it comes quite close to the ontological argument for the existence of God, which has a long and honorable history.

21. See, for example, "The Dynamical Theory of the Intuitions," p. 355:

Writers who make haste to deny the sufficiency of reason in matters of faith, who believe in prayer, and in the communion of the Holy Ghost, when they give the ground of their belief in God often depend solely upon the mind's own laws, or, worse still, upon the mind's own inference from nature, and are slow to recognize the possibility that He who is the finisher of their faith may also be the author of it.

22. "Professor Harris's Contribution to Theism," p. 135.

23. "Orthodox Rationalism," p. 296.

24. "Professor Harris's Contribution to Theism," p. 142.

25. Ibid., pp. 143, 139.

26. Ibid., p. 144.

27. Josiah Royce, "Present Ideals of American University Life," *Scribner's Magazine* 10 (1892): 383.

28. Jane Dewey, ed., "Biography of John Dewey," p. 15 (see chap. 1, n. 1).

29. Actually, there is a third possibility here, the one that Caird and other British Hegelians used in leaving a place for psychology. Like Hegel himself, they drew a distinction between the self as the transcendental ego, the condition of all knowledge and being, the study of which is metaphysics; and the empirical self, the one that occurs with the rest of the world in time and space, the study of which is psychology. Dewey, however, as we shall see in the next chapter, rejected this distinction explicitly in his article "Psychology as Philosophic Method" in *Mind*, the British journal of psychology and philosophy.

There he argued that this latter study of the self as object in the world reduced to pure physiology. And, as we shall see, the terms of Dewey's commitment to psychology, what he wanted out of it, would not let him become a mere natural scientist. He wanted *both* an empirical or experiential base *and* his identity as a philosopher: he was not a scientist, after empiricism for its own sake, but a philosopher-apologist wanting to turn empiricism to the support of "spiritual truth."

For these reasons, then, and in the hope of retaining some slight readability in the text, I am treating this *tertium* as if it did not exist. As Dewey made clear, it didn't exist for him. See John Dewey, "Psychology as Philosophic Method," *Mind* 11 (April 1886): 153–73; *EW 1*, pp. 144–67.

30. Smyth, "Orthodox Rationalism," pp. 310–11.

31. That is to say, just as interaction between ourselves and our natural environment gradually inculcates in us such constitutional truths as "Everything has a cause" or the mathematical axioms, so does interaction between ourselves and our spiritual environment (God's working on us) reveal to us such constitutional theological truths as "There is a God."

32. Smyth, "Orthodox Rationalism," p. 299.

33. Dewey, "The New Psychology," p. 60. Italics mine. Compare this with Smyth's phrasing: "This better method may be described as a thoroughly ethical method" ("Orthodox Rationalism," p. 312).

34. Smyth, "Professor Harris's Contribution to Theism," p. 145. For the antithesis of this (and for an insight into Morris's problems and Dewey's difficulties in this period) recall George Sylvester Morris's Manichaeanism:

> The water-spider provides for its respiration and life beneath the surface of the water by spinning around itself an envelope large enough to contain the air it needs. So we have need, while walking through the thick and often polluted moral atmosphere of this lower world, where seeming life is too frequently inward death, to maintain around ourselves the purer atmosphere of a higher faith. [Morris, "The Immortality of the Soul," *Bibliotheca Sacra* 33 (1876): 715.]

35. Smyth, "Professor Harris's Contribution to Theism," pp. 145–46.

4. Psychology

1. *Calendar of the University of Michigan*, 1885–89. See also George Dykhuizen, *The Life and Mind of John Dewey*, pp. 44 ff. (see chap. 1, n. 1).

2. The Student Christian Association was open to members of the evangelical churches—the Presbyterian, Congregationalist, Baptist, and so forth.

3. John Dewey, "The Obligation to Knowledge of God," *Student Christian Association Monthly Bulletin* 6 (November 1884); *EW 1*, p. 61.

4. Ibid., pp. 62, 63.

5. *Michigan Argonaut*, 18 October 1884.

6. The publications referred to are: John Dewey, *Psychology* (New York: Harper & Bros., 1887); *EW 2*. The book actually was brought out in late 1886, and Dewey had probably completed the manuscript in early 1886. The associated articles were "The Psychological Standpoint," *Mind* 11 (January 1886): 1–19; *EW 1*, pp. 122–43; "Psychology as Philosophic Method," ibid. (April 1886): 153–73; *EW 1*, pp. 144–67; and "Soul and Body," *Bibliotheca Sacra* 43 (April 1886): 239–63; *EW 1*, pp. 93–115. The two articles Dewey wrote

on psychology the following year were "Review of George Trumbull Ladd, *Elements of Physiological Psychology*," *New Englander and Yale Review* 46 (June 1887): 528-37; *EW 1*, pp. 194-204; and "Knowledge as Idealisation," *Mind* 12 (July 1887): 382-96: *EW 1*, pp. 176-93.

7. Dewey to William James, 3 June 1891, quoted in Ralph Barton Perry, *The Thought and Character of William James*, 2:518 (see chap. 2, n. 30).

8. G. Stanley Hall, review of Dewey's *Psychology*, *American Journal of Psychology* 1 (1887): 156. Hall really had blood in his eye: he opined that Dewey's book "might have been written half a century ago" and have "been poorer only by a number of pat physiological illustrations" (ibid., p. 157). All this might be true, but in his decision—once he had begun to call himself a philosophical and experimental psychologist—to spend his time and energies outside the laboratory end of it, Dewey was in good company. William James wrote to his friend, Theodore Flournoy,

> You philosophize, according to your own account, more spontaneously than you work in the laboratory. So do I, and I always felt that the occupation of philosophizing was with me a valid excuse for neglecting laboratory work, since there is not time for both. Your work as a philosopher will be more *irreplaceable* than what results you might get in the laboratory out of the same number of hours. [William James to Theodore Flournoy, 19 September 1892, quoted in Henry James, *Letters of William James*, 2 vols. (Boston, 1920), 1: 325.]

9. Newman Smyth, "Professor Harris's Contribution to Theism," *Andover Review* 1 (1884): 143.

10. Universal, that is, in the sense of a "term that can be applied throughout the universe," the concept itself corresponding to the real nature of things.

11. Dewey, "The New Psychology," *EW 1*, p. 59.

12. Dewey, "Psychology as Philosophic Method," *EW 1*, p. 152.

13. Ibid., pp. 145-46.

14. The two articles are "The Psychological Standpoint" and "Psychology as Philosophic Method" (see above, n. 6).

15. "Psychology as Philosophic Method," p. 150.

16. Ibid., p. 151.

17. See Shadworth H. Hodgson, "Illusory Psychology," *Mind* 11 (1886): 478-94. William James to S. H. Hodgson, 15 March 1887, quoted in Perry, *Thought and Character of William James*, 1:641.

18. "Psychology as Philosophic Method," pp. 163 ff.

19. Ibid., p. 164.

20. Ibid., p. 149.

21. Ibid., p. 157. Italics mine.

22. Quoted in Perry, *Thought and Character of William James*, 2:516.

23. *Psychology*, Preface; *EW 2*, pp. 3-4.

24. James Rowland Angell, in Carl Murchison et al., eds., *History of Psychology in Autobiography*, 5 vols. (Worcester: Clark University Press, 1936), 3:5.

25. Dewey's *Psychology*, needless to say, was not the only one to have trouble here. See James's *Principles of Psychology*, 2 vols. (New York: Henry Holt & Co., 1890), passim.

26. H. A. P. Torrey, review of Dewey's *Psychology*, *Andover Review* 9 (1888): 441.

27. Quoted in Jane Dewey, ed., "Biography of John Dewey," p. 19 (see above, chap. 1, n. 1).

5. Ethics

1. John Dewey, "Ethics in the University of Michigan," *Ethical Record* 2 (October 1889): 145–48; *EW 3*, pp. 48–50. The *Ethical Record* was supplanted by the *International Journal of Ethics* a year later.

2. The commencement address was "Poetry and Philosophy," which he gave at Smith College in June 1890 and published in the *Andover Review* the following summer (*EW 3*, pp. 110–24).

3. Thereafter, in the ensuing decade at Chicago, he did the bulk of his publishing in journals for professional educators and in the professional journals devoted to his university subjects, philosophy and psychology.

4. Dewey, "Ethics in the University of Michigan," *EW 3*, p. 50.

5. Although Dewey's circumstances and his eventual solutions to the problem of putting ethics on a scientific basis were unique, the general problem was not. For a parallel story see David B. Potts, "Social Ethics at Harvard, 1881–1931," in Paul H. Buck, ed., *Social Sciences at Harvard, 1860–1920* (Cambridge: Harvard University Press, 1965), pp. 91–128. See also Jurgen Herbst, *The German Historical School in American Scholarship* (Ithaca: Cornell University Press, 1965), passim.

6. Dewey, "Ethics and Physical Science," *Andover Review* 7 (June 1887): 573–91; *EW 1*, pp. 205–26. In this chapter and in chapter 4, I have for organizational reasons made the distinction between psychology and ethics much sharper than it in fact was in Dewey's work. As C. Stanley Hall pointed out in his review of Dewey's *Psychology* (see chap. 4, n. 8), the book was in many ways an "ethics." Correspondingly, Dewey's second book on ethics, the 1894 *Study of Ethics: A Syllabus*, reads in large part like a treatise on behavioral psychology.

7. Dewey, "Ethics and Physical Science," *EW 1*, p. 209.

8. Ibid., p. 215. Italics mine.

9. Ibid., p. 214.

10. John Dewey, *Outlines of a Critical Theory of Ethics* (Ann Arbor: Inland Press, 1891); *EW 3*, pp. 239–388.

11. Ibid., *EW 3*, p. 300. Lest this sound either self-evident or crass to the reader, it should be noted that it was an extremely economical phrasing of the outcome of a long piece of philosophizing. Dewey appended to the statement the following clarification:

> This satisfied self is found neither in the getting of a lot of pleasures through the satisfaction of desires just as they happen to arise, nor in obedience to law simply because it is law. It is found in satisfaction of desires according to law. This law, however, is not something external to the desires, but is their own law. Each desire is only one striving of character for larger action, and the only way in which it can really find satisfaction (that is, pass from inward striving into outward action) is as a manifestation of character. A desire, taken as a desire for its own apparent or direct end only, is an abstraction. It is a desire for an entire and continuous activity, and its satisfaction requires that

it be fitted into this entire and continuous activity; that it be made con-
formable to the conditions which will bring the whole man into action. It
is this fitting-in which is the law of the desire—the "universal" controlling its
particular nature. (Pp. 300-301.)

12. Ibid., p. 320.

13. Dewey's definitive phrasing reads as follows:

The ethical postulate, the presupposition involved in conduct, is this: IN THE
REALIZATION OF INDIVIDUALITY THERE IS FOUND ALSO THE NEEDED REALIZATION OF
SOME COMMUNITY OF PERSONS OF WHICH THE INDIVIDUAL IS A MEMBER: AND,
CONVERSELY, THE AGENT WHO DULY SATISFIES THE COMMUNITY IN WHICH HE
SHARES, BY THAT SAME CONDUCT SATISFIES HIMSELF. [Ibid., p. 322.]

14. Ibid.

15. Dewey to James Rowland Angell, 10 May 1893, James Rowland Angell
Papers, Sterling Library, Yale University.

16. Dewey, *Outlines*, *EW 3*, p. 323.

17. Felix Adler, "The Freedom of Ethical Fellowship," *International Journal
of Ethics* 1 (October 1890): 16-30; William M. Salter, "A Service of Ethics to
Philosophy," ibid., pp. 114-19.

18. Dewey, "Moral Theory and Practice," *International Journal of Ethics* 1
(January 1891): 186-203; *EW 3*, pp. 93-109.

19. Salter, "A Service of Ethics to Philosophy," p. 116.

20. Dewey, "Moral Theory and Practice," p. 94.

21. Ibid., pp. 94-95.

22. Ibid., pp. 105-6. Dewey used the same example of "the horse-car
conductor" in the *Outlines* book.

23. Nor were his contemporaries slow to point them out. See, especially,
Thomas Davidson's delightful review of the *Outlines* in *Philosophical Review* 1
(1892): 95-99.

24. Salter, "A Service of Ethics to Philosophy," p. 116.

25. Dewey, "Moral Theory and Practice," p. 107.

26. See, for instance, Dewey's remark in this same article: "Besides intelligence, I see but two means of moral emergence: that of hortatory preaching and
that of some scheme as panacea" (p. 104).

27. Perhaps what he is relying on here is the "moral experience" that "verifies"
the postulate. His idea of human moral history, then, would be that through the
centuries men progressively come to postulate (or gamble on) wider and wider
extensions of the core postulate that the common good is identical with the
personal goods of the individuals who make up the society. Before Greek
civilization the postulate had hardly been made at all, and the individual good
was utterly subordinated to the common good (conceived of as the perpetuation
of the ruling dynasty). Then, with the Greeks, the good of the *citizen* was made a
criterion for ascertaining whether the common good was being effected. With
the coming of Christianity, the distinction between slave and citizen was erased,
and the "gamble" was made of insisting that the good of *all* individuals be held
up as a touchstone for the "common good." In each stage the postulate was borne
out, and "moral experience" confirmed that the wider extension of the notion of
the common good was a wise one: life *was* better for all concerned.

As a matter of fact this scheme jibes very closely with the type of Hegelian history Dewey was presenting in the classrooms at Michigan in these years. (See Edwin Peck's notes on Dewey's course, "Movements of Thought in the Nineteenth Century [1893–94]," Edwin Peck Papers, Michigan Historical Collections, University of Michigan, Ann Arbor.)

28. Dewey, "Moral Theory and Practice," p. 101.

29. This is one example of the Hegelian influence, and particularly relevant to our discussion here. His ethical doctrine derived from the Hegelians in numerous other ways also, and Dewey was quite ready to enumerate them. See, for example, his preface to *Outlines of a Critical Theory of Ethics.*

30. Dewey, "Moral Theory and Practice," p. 109.

31. Dewey, "Green's Theory of the Moral Motive," *Philosophical Review* 1 (November 1892): 593–612; *EW 3*, pp. 155–73; and "Self-Realization as the Moral Ideal," ibid. 2 (November 1893): 652–64; *EW 4*, pp. 42–53.

32. After "The Psychological Standpoint" and "Psychology as Philosophic Method," both published in *Mind* in 1886, and his 1887 defense of his position against S. H. Hodgson's attack (see S. H. Hodgson, "Illusory Psychology," *Mind* 9 [October 1886]: 478–94; reprinted in *EW 1*, xli–xvii), Dewey published two other articles in the British journal, both pursuant of the themes of his earlier articles. The first article was "Knowledge as Idealisation" (*Mind* 12 [July 1887]; *EW 1*, pp. 176–93). The second article, "On Some Current Conceptions of the Term 'Self' " (*Mind* 15 [January 1890], 58–74; *EW 3*, pp. 57–74) is one of the more difficult pieces Dewey wrote, but its thrust is to make the self and the world-as-experienced identical, which would presumably have the effect of making the self not mysterious and transcendental but rather potentially intelligible by (scientific) "method."

33. See, for instance, "Moral Theory and Practice":

Any being who is capable of acting from ideas—that is, whose conduct is the attempted realization of proposed ends—must conceive of these ends in terms of something to be done—of obligation. And that is what is meant by saying not only that the "ought" rests upon and expresses the "is," but that it is itself the "is" of action. What we ordinarily call an "is" is simply the "is" of fact at rest. If action, or the following out of ideas, is not a fact, with just the same claims to be considered a part of the real world as a stick or a stone, a planet, or an earthworm, then, and then only, have Mr. Salter's remarks about the separation of the "is" and the "ought," the unverifiableness of moral ideas, the attractiveness and authority of moral ideas apart from facts, and the existence of a domain beyond science, any shred of meaning. [P. 109.]

34. Ibid., p. 108.

35. Again, his formula at that time: Psychology is to be studied by empirics; metaphysics is to be studied by psychology; therefore....

36. John Dewey, "The Place of Religious Emotion," *Monthly Bulletin* (Student Christian Association) 8 (November 1886); *EW 1*, p. 91.

37. Sidney Hook, "Some Memories of John Dewey," *Commentary* 14 (1952): 246.

38. Dewey, "Moral Theory and Practice," pp. 103–4.

39. Ibid., p. 100.

40. Dewey, *Outlines of Ethics*, p. 377. The quote continued:

To cease this activity is not to remain on the attained level, for that, *when attained*, was active. It is to relapse, to slip down into badness. The moral end is always an activity. To fail in this activity is, therefore, to involve character in disintegration. It can be kept together only by constant organizing activity; only by acting upon new wants and moving towards new situations. Let this activity cease, and disorganization ensues, as surely as the body decays when life goes, instead of simply remaining inert as it was. Bad conduct is thus *unprincipled*; it has no center, no movement. The good man is "organic"; he uses his attainments to discover new needs, and to assimilate new material. He lives from within outwards, his character is compact, coherent; he has *integrity*. The bad man, having no controlling unity, has no consistent line of action; his motives of conduct contradict one another; he follows this maxim in relation to this person, that in relation to another; character is *demoralized*. The bad man is unstable and double-minded. He is not one person, but a group of conflicting wills. [Pp. 377–78.]

The reader will note the similarity of the behavior model of Dewey's good man to the model of the good working scientist and his progress: "The good man is 'organic'; he uses his attainments to discover new needs, and to assimilate new material," and so forth.

41. George Sylvester Morris, "The Philosophy of Art," *Journal of Speculative Philosophy* 10 (1876): 11.

42. Dewey to William James, 10 May 1891, quoted in Ralph Barton Perry, *The Thought and Character of William James*, 2:517 (see chap. 2, n. 28).

43. Delos F. Wilcox to Frank Manny, 23 May 1895, Frank Manny Papers, Michigan Historical Collections, University of Michigan, Ann Arbor.

44. John Dewey, Review of S. Bryant, *Studies in Character, Psychological Review* 3 (1896): 218–22; *EW* 5, p. 352.

45. Dewey to Thomas A. Davidson, 14 March 1891, Thomas A. Davidson Papers, Sterling Library, Yale University.

46. Ibid.

47. John Dewey and James Hayden Tufts, *Ethics* (New York: Holt, 1908), p. 298.

48. John Dewey, *The Public and Its Problems* (New York: Holt, 1927), pp. 154–55.

49. Randolph Bourne, "Twilight of Idols," *Seven Arts* 2 (October 1917): 696.

6. Publics, Politics

1. *Michigan Argonaut*, University of Michigan, 1 November 1884, quoted in Willinda Savage, "The Evolution of John Dewey's Philosophy of Experimentalism as Developed at the University of Michigan" (Ph.D. diss., University of Michigan, 1950), p. 74.

2. W. P. Robinson, "Ponying at the University of Michigan," *Monthly Bulletin* (Student Christian Association, University of Michigan) 4 (December 1893): 89; quoted in Savage, "Evolution of John Dewey's Philosophy," p. 80.

3. Charles H. Cooley, *Sociological Theory and Social Research* (New York: Holt, 1930), p. 6.

4. Delos F. Wilcox to Frank Manny, 25 July 1894, 18 January 1895, and 30 April 1895, Frank Manny Papers, Michigan Historical Collections, University of Michigan, Ann Arbor.

5. Interview of Miss Jessie Phelps by Willinda Savage, 19 January 1950, quoted in Savage, "Evolution of John Dewey's Philosophy," p. 137.

6. Dewey, "Christianity and Democracy," in *Religious Thought at the University of Michigan* (Ann Arbor: Register Publishing Co., Inland Press, 1893), pp. 60–69; *EW 4*, pp. 4–5.

7. Hugh Hawkins, *Pioneer: A History of The Johns Hopkins University, 1874–1889* (Ithaca: Cornell University Press, 1960).

8. Dewey, *The Ethics of Democracy*, University of Michigan Philosophical Papers, 2d ser., no. 1 (Ann Arbor: Andrews & Co., 1888), 28 pp.; *EW 1*, p. 246.

9. Hattie Alice Chipman was a month older than Dewey. She had been a student at the University of Michigan with a special interest in philosophy when Dewey came to the university. She took several of his courses, and they first met socially at a boardinghouse where they both took their meals. They were married in July 1886.

10. Mabel Castle to Henry Northrup Castle, 31 December 1893, Henry Northrup Castle Papers, University of Chicago Library.

11. Mabel Castle to Castle parents, 24 December 1893, Castle Papers.

12. Mabel Castle to Henry Northrup Castle, 6 December 1893, Castle Papers.

13. Helen Castle Mead to her mother, 30 July 1894, Castle Papers.

14. Henry Northrup Castle to parents, 10 June 1893, Castle Papers.

15. Jane Dewey, ed., "Biography of John Dewey," p. 21 (see above, chap. 1, n. 1).

16. We know of Franklin Ford and his brother Corydon largely through their contact with Dewey and through their few publications. See, especially, Franklin Ford, *Draft of Action* ("This is printed, not published. It is to be held in confidence"; ca. 1892; copy in Michigan Historical Collections, University of Michigan, Ann Arbor), and Corydon Ford, *The Child of Democracy or the Embryo State* (New York: Intelligence Company of America, 1893), *The Child of Democracy: Being the Adventures of the Embryo State: 1856–1894* (Ann Arbor: John V. Sheehan & Co., 1894), and *The Synthesis of Mind: The Method of a Working Psychology* (1893).

17. Franklin Ford, *Draft of Action*, p. 16.

18. Ibid., pp. 2–3.

19. Corydon Ford, *The Child of Democracy: Being the Adventures of the Embryo State*, p. 174.

20. Dewey to Henry Carter Adams, 29 April 1889, Henry Carter Adams Papers, Michigan Historical Collections, University of Michigan, Ann Arbor.

21. Such etymological play fascinated Dewey during his days with Ford.

22. "Memorandum" enclosed in Dewey to Henry Carter Adams, 29 April 1889, Adams Papers.

23. Dewey, "The Present Position of Logical Theory," *Monist* 2 (October 1891): 1–17; *EW 3*, pp. 125–41.

24. Ibid., p. 139.

25. Ibid., p. 140.

26. Dewey, "Poetry and Philosophy," *Andover Review* 16 (August 1891): 105–16; *EW 3*, p. 123.

27. Dewey, "The Present Position of Logical Theory," *EW 3*, p. 140.

28. *Inlander* (University of Michigan), as quoted in Willinda Savage, "John Dewey and 'Thought News' at the University of Michigan," *Michigan Quarterly Review* 56 (spring 1950): 208.

29. "The Present Position of Logical Theory," *EW 3*, p. 123.

30. Dewey, "The Scholastic and the Speculator," *Inlander* 2 (December 1891): 145–48; ibid. (January 1892): 186–88; *EW* 3, pp. 148–54.

31. Ibid., pp. 150–51.

32. Dewey to James Rowland Angell, 11 March 1892, James Rowland Angell Papers, Sterling Library, Yale University.

33. Dewey to Thomas A. Davidson, Thomas A. Davidson Papers, Sterling Library, Yale University.

34. *Detroit Tribune*, 10 April 1892.

35. Ibid., 13 April 1892.

36. Dewey to Willinda Savage, 30 May 1949, quoted in Savage, "The Evolution of John Dewey's Philosophy," p. 150.

37. Corydon Ford, *The Child of Democracy: Being the Adventures of the Embryo State*, pp. 174–75.

38. Dewey, *Introduction to Philosophy: Syllabus of Course 5* (Philosophical Department, University of Michigan, February 1892), 24 pp.; *EW 3*, pp. 211–35.

39. Dewey, "How Do Concepts Arise from Percepts?" *Public-School Journal* 11 (November 1891): 128–30; *EW 3*, p. 146.

40. Corydon Ford, *The Child of Democracy: Being the Adventures . . .*, p. 134.

41. *Inlander*, as quoted in Willinda Savage, "John Dewey and 'Thought News' at the University of Michigan," p. 208.

42. *Detroit Tribune*, 13 April 1892.

43. George Herbert Mead, "The Definition of the Psychical," *University of Chicago Decennial Publications*, 1st ser., 10 vols. (Chicago: University of Chicago Press, 1903), 3:100.

7. George Herbert Mead

1. Henry Northrup Castle, *Letters* (London, 1902).

2. Henry Northrup Castle to Mabel Castle, 20 January 1895, Henry Northrup Castle Papers, University of Chicago Library.

3. George Herbert Mead to Henry Northrup Castle, 28 February 1884, George Herbert Mead Papers, University of Chicago Library.

4. Mead to Castle, 19 July 1883, Mead Papers.

5. Mead to Castle, 12 March 1884, Mead Papers.

6. Mead to Castle, undated, Mead Papers.

7. Mead to Castle, 7 March 1884, Mead Papers.

8. Mead to Castle, 5 March 1884, Mead Papers.

9. As it turned out, he need not have worried about his mother. She became president of Mount Holyoke College in 1890.

10. Castle to his parents, 25 July 1886, Castle Papers.

11. Mead to Castle, 30 November 1885, Mead Papers.

12. Mead to Castle, 16 May 1886, Mead Papers.

13. Mead to Castle, 14 April 1887, 15 November 1883, Mead Papers.

14. Mead to Castle, 28 February 1886, Mead Papers.

15. Henry Castle to Helen Castle, 24 March 1889, Castle Papers.

16. Mead to Castle, 28 February 1886, Mead Papers.
17. Mead to Castle, 18 September 1884, Mead Papers.
18. Mead to Castle, 16 March 1884, Mead Papers.
19. Mead to Castle, 16 August 1884, Mead Papers.
20. Mead to Castle, 8 February 1885, 22 February 1885, 30 March 1885, Mead Papers.
21. Mead to Castle, 28 October 1886, 26 April 1887, 29 April 1887, 5 May 1887, Mead Papers.
22. Castle to Mead, 30 July 1887, Castle Papers. Italics in original.
23. Josiah Royce, *The Spirit of Modern Philosophy* (Boston and New York: Houghton Mifflin, 1892), p. 115.
24. "Josiah Royce—A Personal Impression," *International Journal of Ethics* 27 (1916–17): 169.
25. Josiah Royce, *Spirit of Modern Philosophy*, pp. 116–17.
26. Mead, "Josiah Royce," pp. 169–70.
27. Henry Castle to Helen Castle, 9 October 1887, Castle Papers.
28. Mead to Castle, 19 June 1888, Mead Papers.
29. Mead to Castle, 1 July 1888, Mead Papers.
30. Mead to Castle, 18 July 1888, Mead Papers. The full text of Mead's remarks about Santayana reads:

James read me a letter from Santiana. He is discouraged and disheartened with philosophy calls Wundt a survival of the Alchemist and does [not] see any prospect of getting anything more abroad and wants to use his fellowship at Harvard next year. Says he may develop out of his disgust a system if he has sufficient audacity to, and means to do this next year, I believe. James thinks he lacks the virile dogged qualities which make the successful worker in this or any direction.

Santayana's letter to James is quoted in part in Perry, *Thought and Character of William James*, 1:405–6.

31. Mead to Castle, 6 May 1887, Mead Papers.
32. Actually, such work appears not to have been that much further along even in Europe. "Physiological Psychology is a science as yet very much in the air which has hardly materialized yet, and poor George is utterly at a loss how to begin. Every Professor we visited here had a different piece of advice to impart, and to match those different pieces together would have baffled the ingenuity of a Chinese puzzle manufacturer" (Henry Castle to parents, 3 February 1889, Castle Papers).
33. Castle to parents, 3 February 1889, Castle Papers.
34. Castle to parents, 15 February 1888, Castle Papers.
35. Henry Castle to Helen Castle, 24 March 1889, Castle Papers.
36. Castle to parents, 26 March 1889; to Mead, 31 March 1889, Castle Papers.
37. Castle to parents, 7 April 1889, Castle Papers.
38. Henry Castle to Helen Castle, 24 June 1889, Castle Papers.
39. Cf. Mead to Castle, undated August 1890, quoted below, p. 130.
40. Castle to Mead, 24 October 1889, Castle Papers.
41. Referred to in Castle to Mead, 8 January 1890, Castle Papers.
42. Mead to Castle, undated, and 29 September 1890, Mead Papers.

43. Mead to Castle, undated, 1890, Mead Papers.
44. Mead, "Josiah Royce," p. 168.
45. Mead to Castle, undated August or September, 1890, Mead Papers. The next several quotes are from this letter.
46. Mead to Castle, undated August 1890, Mead Papers.
47. Mead to Castle, 21 October 1890, Mead Papers.
48. Ibid.
49. Castle to parents, 24 November 1890, Castle Papers.
50. Castle to parents, 10 June 1891, Castle Papers.
51. Mead to Castle, 22 July 1891, Mead Papers.
52. Mead to Castle, 20 October 1891, Mead Papers.
53. Ibid.
54. Ibid.

8. The Emergence of Dewey's Pragmatism

1. John Dewey, Introduction to Philosophy: Syllabus of Course 5; EW 3, pp. 211–35. Corydon Ford apparently took this course and then published his notes on it as The Synthesis of Mind: The Method of a Working Psychology (1893). See above, chap. 6, n. 16.
2. John Dewey to James Rowland Angell, 11 March 1892, James Rowland Angell Papers, Sterling Library, Yale University.
3. Introduction to Philosophy: Syllabus, EW 3, p. 211. All the quotations in the next several paragraphs are from pages 212–13 of the Syllabus.
4. Dewey, "The Reflex Arc Concept in Psychology," Psychological Review 3 (July 1896): 357–70; EW 5, pp. 96–109.
5. Dewey to Angell, 25 April 1892, Angell Papers.
6. Dewey to Angell, 10 May 1893, Angell Papers.
7. Dewey, "The Reflex Arc Concept in Psychology," EW 5, p. 97.
8. Ibid., p. 98.
9. Ibid.
10. Ibid., pp. 99–100.
11. Ibid., pp. 103–4.
12. Ibid., p. 106. Italics Dewey's.
13. Dewey would have us notice that the ordinary pairings of sensation with stimulus and movement with response are another mistake in the reflex-arc formulation. In the first stage of the sequence we are discussing, for instance, it is the anticipation of the movement, the end of the coordination, that is the stimulus to the child's action of examining the light. Similarly, in the second part of the sequence, the child's attention turns to his arm and to what he has decided is the movement he wishes to make. In his concentration on this, he experiences muscular sensation. So, Dewey concludes, the stimulus and the response are located in different areas in each successive movement of the new coordination.
14. It should be noted here that idealism as an element in Dewey's thought had begun to ebb in the last year or so of the 1880s.
15. George Herbert Mead to Henry Northrup Castle, 19 December 1891, Mead Papers, University of Chicago Library.
16. Mead to Castle, 27 December 1891, Mead Papers.
17. Mead to Castle, undated, Mead Papers.

18. Mead to Castle, 28 February 1892, Mead Papers.
19. Mead, "Josiah Royce—A Personal Impression," *International Journal of Ethics* 27 (1916–17): 168.
20. Mead to Castle, 12 January 1894, Mead Papers.
21. Mead to Castle parents, 18 June 1892, Mead Papers.
22. Mead to Castle parents, 21 August 1892, Mead Papers.
23. Mead to Castle, 29 June 1892, Mead Papers.
24. Mead to Castle parents, 18 June 1892, Mead Papers.

9. The Fruits of Pragmatism

1. George Herbert Mead, review of LeBon's *Psychology of Socialism*, *American Journal of Sociology* 5 (1899): 406. The reader might notice how this doctrine of Mead's serves Dewey's ethical postulate. See chapter 5, above.
2. Mark De Wolfe Howe, ed., *Holmes-Pollock Letters*, 2 vols. (Cambridge: Harvard University Press, 1941), 2:287
3. John Dewey, *Experience and Nature*, 2d ed. (Chicago: Open Court Publishing Co., 1929), p. 2a. (The first edition was published in 1925.)
4. Ibid., p. v.
5. Ibid.
6. Ibid., p. 2.
7. George P. Adams, review in *International Journal of Ethics* 36 (January 1926): 202.
8. Dewey, *Experience and Nature*, p. 43; Adams's review, p. 202.
9. Dewey, *Experience and Nature*, p. 193; Adams's review, p. 203.
10. Dewey, *Experience and Nature*, pp. 78–79.
11. Hall's ambition became grasping and even paranoid. See Dorothy Ross, *G. Stanley Hall*, passim (see chap. 2, n. 23).
12. Dewey, "Social Science and Social Control," *New Republic* 67 (29 July 1931): 277.
13. Adams, review of *Experience and Nature*, p. 204. See also Barry Karl, *Executive Reorganization and Reform in the New Deal* (Cambridge: Harvard University Press, 1963), passim.
14. Paul Bourke, "The Social Critics and the End of American Innocence: 1907–1921," *Journal of American Studies* 3 (1060): 57–72.
15. Ibid., p. 70.
16. Randolph Bourne, "Twilight of Idols," *Seven Arts* 2 (October 1917): 691.
17. Ibid., p. 698.
18. The same criticism of Dewey's philosophy had been posed in the *Seven Arts* some months earlier by Van Wyck Brooks in an essay titled "Our Awakeners" (*Seven Arts* 2 [May 1917]: 235–48), but in much calmer terms. Paul Bourke has argued convincingly that it was Brooks's critique that gave focus to Bourne's feeling of betrayal. See Paul Bourke, "The Status of Politics 1909–1919: *The New Republic*, Randolph Bourne, and Van Wyck Brooks," *Journal of American Studies* 8 (1974): 171–202.
19. Bourne, "Twilight of Idols," pp. 692, 689, 695.
20. Ibid., pp. 696–97.
21. Ibid., p. 697.
22. Ibid.

Bibliographical Note

As recently as eight years ago, writing about the young John Dewey involved an inordinate amount of legwork. Milton Halsey Thomas's *John Dewey: A Centennial Bibliography* (Chicago: University of Chicago Press, 1962) was then, as now, an invaluable guide to Dewey's published writings, but the writings themselves were difficult to obtain. The articles and essays had been published in a variety of periodicals, many of them now defunct. First or unrevised editions of the early books were very hard to find; tracing their revisions in succeeding editions, all but impossible. Dewey's unpublished writings and what had survived of his correspondence and personal papers were scattered and difficult of access.

Happily, that has all changed. The Center for Dewey Studies at Southern Illinois University, founded in 1961, has brought out a definitive five-volume edition of the young Dewey's extant published work, *John Dewey: The Early Works, 1882-1898* (Carbondale: Southern Illinois University Press, 1967-72; paperback ed., 1975), and will shortly begin to bring out a second series, of fifteen volumes, covering the work of the next period in his life, "The Middle Works of John Dewey, 1898-1924." The Center has also published a useful topical guide to Dewey's immense corpus, *Guide to the Works of John Dewey*, edited by Jo Ann Boydston (Carbondale: Southern Illinois University Press, 1970; paperback, 1974). Further, the Center has functioned as the central archive for Dewey's work, collecting there the bulk of his surviving personal papers and working in cooperation with other individuals and libraries throughout the world to locate and organize Dewey's published work, his correspondence, and related materials.

I have kept to a minimum in the body of this book references to predecessors who have written about young Dewey. Their books and articles, however, have been present to my work, and I should mention and commend to the reader at least those whose work bore most directly on my own. Lewis Feuer has written two delightful articles interpreting this period of Dewey's life, "H. A. P. Torrey and John Dewey: Teacher and Pupil," *American Quarterly* 10 (1958): 34-54, and "John Dewey and the Back-to-the-People Movement in American Thought," *Journal of the History of Ideas* 20 (1959): 545-68. The latter article, especially, suggests a valuable perspective on Dewey. Morton White's *The Origin of Dewey's Instrumentalism* (New York: Columbia University Press, 1943) addresses the same period in Dewey's life as does my book. I think our work can be distinguished fairly by saying that his is a philosopher's inquiry while mine is more an intellectual historian's, since it asks more insistently *why* Dewey thought what he thought and often goes outside philosophy to find the answer.

Dewey scholarship has lately been blessed with a full scholarly biography of the philosopher, George Dykhuizen's *The Life and Mind of John Dewey* (Carbondale: Southern Illinois University Press, 1973). Professor Dykhuizen sensed the need for a well-researched, straightforward account of Dewey's life and work, and his book will lend encouragement and secure footing to more interpretive efforts, such as mine.

There are numerous other items I might mention: Willinda Savage's unpublished dissertation, "The Evolution of John Dewey's Philosophy of Experimentalism as Developed at the University of Michigan" (University of Michigan, 1950), the fine little introductory essays at the beginning of each volume of *The Early Works of John Dewey*, Darnell Rucker's *The Chicago Pragmatists* (Minneapolis: University of Minnesota Press, 1969), and so forth. Suffice it to say that the secondary literature on Dewey is vast. As a guide to it the Center for Dewey Studies has recently published *Checklist of Writings about John Dewey*, edited by Jo Ann Boydston and Kathleen Poulos (Carbondale: Southern Illinois University Press, 1974).

Index